# The Mediaeval Castles
# of Skye and Lochalsh

ROGER MIKET AND DAVID L. ROBERTS

# The Mediaeval Castles
# of Skye and Lochalsh

BIRLINN

*Previous page.* Low relief from a ? fireplace-
surround, found at Duntulm Castle by Murdo
A. Nicolson amongst rubble from the jamb
which collapsed in January 1990. ? earlier 17th
century. Height 190mm.

First published by MacLean Press in 1990
This edition published in 2007 by
Birlinn Limited
West Newington House
10 Newington Road
Edinburgh
EH9 1QS

www.birlinn.co.uk

ISBN13: 978 1 84158 613 7
ISBN10: 1 84158 613 7

British Library Cataloguing-in-Publication Data
A catalogue record for this book is available
from the British Library

Designed and typeset by Mark Blackadder

Printed and bound by
Antony Rowe Ltd, Chippenham

# Contents

*For Ian Begg;*
*Architect in the Scottish Tradition*

# Foreword

This volume fills a void in the literature dealing with this part of the world, and will be welcomed both by those resident in the area, and by those whose interest has been awakened by holidaying here. As a scholarly, yet approachable dissertation upon the Castles of Skye and Lochalsh, it is most interesting on many different levels.

None of the castles discussed here preserves the aspect of their 'original' creation because the conditions under which they were first built bear no relation to the conditions of the present day. They were necessary in reflection of Man's constant need in a hostile world to defend himself and, as that world has changed, as weapons have altered from swords and spears to guns and bombs, so have the castles metamorphosed – some, their raison d'etre removed, dwindling into a more or less defined heap of stones.

It is said that the pen is mightier than the sword, but against the sword of this book, these castles do not need to defend themselves. Instead they are resurrected in their ancient reality, or realities. It is good to try to understand the past and, in struggling to defend our own lives in this modern world, honour our forefathers' efforts to do the same in theirs.

I welcome the contribution that this book makes to that understanding, and I wish it well.

*Macleod*

*John MacLeod of MacLeod*

# Acknowledgements

Preparation of this booklet has drawn heavily upon the advice and support of many individuals and institutions. Without the historical advice of Dr Alasdair MacLean, Geoffrey Stell of the Royal Commission on the Ancient and Historical Monuments of Scotland (RCAHMS), and Christopher Tabraham of Historic Buildings and Monuments and Alison Sheridan of the National Museum of Scotland, the text would be immeasurably the poorer. In the preparation of the line illustrations we are grateful to Martin Wildgoose, George Kozikowski and Graham Parry for their help with the plans of *Caisteal Maol* and Dun Ringill. Illustrations lent or authorized by institutions are acknowledged where appropriate. It is a pleasure to thank John MacLeod of MacLeod, now the only chief to live in the family castle, for writing the foreword.

# Introduction

Like the brochs of an earlier epoch the castles of the district are the monuments of an age otherwise only illuminated by documents and tradition. Archaeology has yet to reveal, from the clusters of small homesteads scattered around the coastline, how the majority lived, dependent upon the land and sea for their livelihood. The castles alone remain as the only prominent landscape evidence of a great age in West Highland history. Though all but two of the ten castles within the district now lie in desolate ruin, between the 12th and 15th centuries these fortified residences were the hub of social, political and economic order for a society whose allegiances were shaped by the family or kin. Such 'families' or clans were identifiable by surnames like MacAskill,

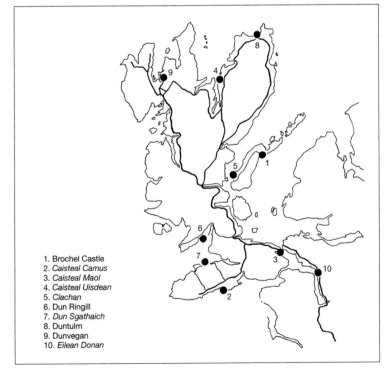

1. Brochel Castle
2. *Caisteal Camus*
3. *Caisteal Maol*
4. *Caisteal Uisdean*
5. *Clachan*
6. Dun Ringill
7. *Dun Sgathaich*
8. Duntulm
9. Dunvegan
10. *Eilean Donan*

Distribution of castles within the district of Skye and Lochalsh. The numbers indicate their order in this guide and the map shows the modern road system.

*Above*. Unfinished boat stem-post from a vessel dated by radiocarbon analysis to between the later 9th and mid-11th centuries AD. Found on the Isle of Eigg, *ante* 1878 (National Museums Scotland).

*Right*. 'Loch na h-airde, Rubha an Dunan (NG 396 159), looking south. The mouth of the canal is visible just to the left of centre, and below the eminence to the left (east) which is capped by the stout wall of the Iron Age 'dun' or fort. It would be surprising indeed were some future excavation not to show re-use of this defensive site in the mediaeval period, presumably by the MacAskills.

MacDonald, MacKinnon and MacLeod. These arose in a political vacuum and a complex system of Gaelic law based on kinship developed to underpin its structure. The foremost member of a clan was its chief. As a protector and preserver of the clan he was assisted and advised by a wide range of dignitaries whose positions, like his own, were usually of an hereditary nature; the position of bard within the household of the MacDonalds of Clanranald for example, was held by the same family for over 18 generations! From the chief's residence spread decisions affecting every clan member, and its shadow was indeed a long one. In the case of the MacLeods a patrimony stretching from Glenelg on the mainland, to remote St. Kilda in the Atlantic, was regulated from Dunvegan's halls.

Something of the relationship between the chiefs of clans rising in power and their immediate neighbours might be drawn from that between the MacLeod's and the MacAskills. Of Scandinavian descent, the MacAskills of Skye had long been resident on Rubha an Dunan, an extensive tongue of land jutting out south-westward from the foot of the Cuillin into the Sea of the Hebrides. Despite its relatively landlocked isolation from the rest of Skye, the peninsula is perfectly situated for access to the sea highway and it was undoubtedly this that attracted the MacAskills, who were acknowledged sea-farers, to settle here. By the early 13th century, the district of Minginish, in which the peninsula lies, passed into the patrimony of the MacLeods. For the MacLeods of

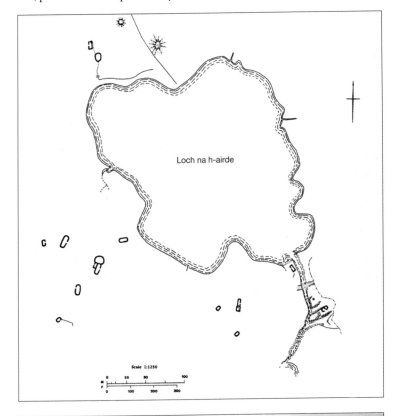

Loch na h-airde

Scale 1:1250

Plan of Loch na h-airde, Rubha an Dunan. The plan shows the position of the two Neolithic burial cairns (4th millennium BC) divided by the stone boundary wall on the northern side of the loch; various sub-rectangular buildings, some with attached enclosures around the loch, and the curving course of the canal at the south-eastern corner with its slipways. (Adam Welfare)

The canal opening onto the sea, with Canna in the distance. The slipways are evident wherever the surprisingly intact side-walls are discontinued.

Dun Troddan, Glenelg (NG 8338 1752). It stood to a height of 13.5m. until 1722, in which year, '... some Goth purloined from the tip, 7 feet and a half, under pretence of applying the materials to certain public buildings'. These 'certain public buildings...' are the 18th century barracks at Bernera, now protected as a Scheduled Ancient Monument in their own right!'

Dunvegan the strategic situation of Rubha an Dunan was critical in both protecting and giving advance notice of any potential sea-threat from this quarter, and for generations thereafter the MacAskills carried out the responsibility for acting as wardens of the coast for the MacLeods. Their later homestead with its archaic one-apsidal end still stands in its enclosure some distance to the east of an extensive inland loch, however it is highly probable that its predecessor was the dun to the south of the loch, sited on an eminence overlooking the sea (NG 396 159). In an island of exceptional archaeological richness, one of its least known but most remarkable monuments is the man-made tidal canal built to connect this loch to the sea (see p.x). The canal is over 100 metres in length, with well-built stone side-walls interrupted here and there for *nuists*, ramps that act as docking places for vessels to be pulled up out of the water. Such elaborate construction points to roles other than simply that of lookouts for the MacLeods, such as specialists in the tasks of construction, repair and maintenance of vessels.

That the situation at Rubha an Dunan was far from exceptional is indicated by the discovery of two unfinished boat end-posts found 20 kilometres away on the isle of Eigg sometime before 1878. Fashioned from oak and reflecting local wood-working techniques,

The two best preserved brochs on the mainland are at Glenelg opposite Skye. In this illustration of 'Dun Telve, Glenelg', made by Moses Griffiths in 1772, are shown the galleries within the walls which may have influenced local response in mediaeval castle design.

they are from a clinker-built fishing or ferry vessel about 10 metres in length and 2 metres in width, and dated by radiocarbon to between 885–1035 AD. There can be little doubt of the advantages of such a 'dockyard' in a Hebridean world dependent upon sea mobility and naval strength. The galley was, after all, the symbol of Clan MacDonald, Lords of the Isles, with Somerled, Lord of the Isles not only having his own fleet of birlinn but also developing the *nyvaig* (little ship). Clinker-built, over 18 metres in length and with a capacity for between 12 and 20 oarsmen on each side, it outclassed earlier Scandinavian designs with its innovation of a single-hinge rudder, rather than being steered by an oar, and a fighting top at the mast-head to improve fire-power. For centuries these were instruments of strength to the chiefs, until made obsolete by manoeuvrable warships with cannon and musket. The island chiefs managed to hang onto their galles until 1616, when a statute forbade the possession of, 'more than one galley or birling of 16 or 18 oars [so] that in their voyage through the isles they should not oppress the Country people'. Less is known of these West Highland vessels than their Scandinavian predecessors and, in the quest to recover at first hand fragments that might inform us, no better place could be thought to exist than that where vessels were constructed and brought for repair than this silted inland loch.

Not all castles within the district were the residences of clan chiefs. Whilst these may have been occupied at various times by relatives, all were in his possession. Whether as a main residence or subsidiary stronghold, these buildings were symbols of the power and prestige of the clan. They functioned as retreats in times of danger, places to feast in, plan attacks from and make alliances, denote military might, cultural centres for encouragement of the arts, a source of news of the world beyond, and at one the touchstone and home of every clan member.

While Dr. Johnson's wry claim that any one of Edward II's Welsh castles might have supplied the materials with which to build every Scottish castle is excessive, those within the district are indeed small by comparison with many southern castles. These were not however the product of a powerful kingship intent on control through a judicious network of garrisoned strongholds. As with the majority of Scottish 'castles', they were little more than fortified residences. However elaborated by successive chiefs, this was a role that none within the district outgrew despite an attempt by the Crown to elevate Caisteal Camus, in the south of the island, to the status of a royal residence. While throughout their lives the purpose of these residences remained unchanged, their origin and evolution is of profound interest. The complex building succession which many sites have undergone, and the sadly ruinous condition of the majority of these strongholds, make an understanding of the evolution of any one site difficult. The castles share a surprisingly wide range of characteristics which indicate that their development lies within the general framework familiar in other parts of Scotland.

> The castles of the Hebrides, many of which are standing, and
> many ruined, were always built upon points of land on the
> margin of sea. For the choice of this situation there must
> have been some general reason, which the change of manners
> has left in obscurity.
> (Samuel Johnson, *A Journey to the Western Islands of Scotland*,
> 1775)

It has been claimed that the 16th-century carving of a castle on the tomb of Alasdair Crotach represents his former residence of Dunvegan. None of the details represented on the carving (e.g. drawbridge, steps on the landward side, and pointed window) occur at Dunvegan. The carving seems rather to be stylized, perhaps from the hand of an Irish craftsman reflected in the stepped merlons not found in Scotland (from K. A. Steer & J. W. M. Bannerman, *Late Medieval Monumental Sculpture in the West Highlands*, HMSO, 1977).

That all the castles lie on the coast is of little surprise given that the population as a whole shared this preference for settlement on the better agricultural land adjacent to the rich harvests from the sea. Moreover, in the absence of roads, the sea has long been the main highway of an island people. Their distribution depended upon the situation and extent of the territory of a particular clan. The chief residence usually lay within the home territory that denoted the sept, or family of the clan, i.e. the MacKinnons of Strathairdle, or the

MacDonalds of Sleat. The chiefs of these two particular clans did, for a short time, remove their main residence outside the home territory, but, given the feuding temperament of the clan, there are no instances of a castle within the territory of one clan falling within the patrimony of another. When transfers of territory took place the castles within were invariably included.

The imprudence of acting otherwise was plain; so it was that, in an attempt to resolve a long-standing dispute between the Mac-Donalds and MacLeods concerning Trotternish, the king stipulated that possession of the castle at Duntulm would signify possession of the territory.

All the castles occupy dominantly defensive situations, usually astride a platform of outcropping rock or at the end of small promontories. In this respect they share much in common with the many earlier Iron Age fortifications built around the coastline – the brochs and duns – showing how similar were the needs of societies separated by over a thousand years. Within the district there does indeed appear to be a striking coincidence between these earlier defences and the mediaeval castles, not fully explained by topography alone. While the visible evidence for an Iron Age phase of occupation has only been observed at Eilean Donan and Dun Ringill, tradition and the frequency of the 'dun' element in the names of many of these castles are strong indications that as many as seven of the ten castles were purposefully situated on sites with a longer history of defensive works.

Though tradition is by itself not necessarily a reliable indicator of antiquity, stories are woven around Caisteal Maol, Duntulm and Dun Sgathaich which refer to settlement there at a date earlier than the visible mediaeval buildings. Caisteal Maol was formerly known as Dunakin, the fort of a Scandinavian king, Haakon, and Duntulm was formerly Dun Dhaibhidh, David reputedly being a Norwegian chief settled here sometime before the mid-13th century. Dun Sgathaich might be considered as the most historic of the castles in the district, for in Celtic heroic tradition it was visited by the legendary Iron Age hero Cú Chulainn, who came here from Ireland to train in the art of warfare. Given the nature of Gaelic tradition, and the ease with which legends were woven around prominent natural features and prehistoric remains in the landscape, many stories might justifiably be regarded with suspicion. Any good story-teller wanting to represent the product of a fertile imagination as a truth would sensibly build it around a landscape familiar to his listeners. When Walter Scott drew *Dun Sgathaich* into 'The Lay of the Last Minstrel', he was using a device already of great antiquity. Yet while the stories themselves might be suspect, they do have an historical point to make, namely that these castles were considered sufficiently ancient in their own right to be a fitting setting for the action: if those listening knew the settlement to have been recent, the whole story would have fallen. That *Dun Sgathaich* and Dunakin are referred to by name in later mediaeval documents clearly shows these traditions to have been already established at the time.

Perhaps the most significant indication that a mediaeval castle might overlie an earlier fortification is the use of the term 'dun' in a castle's name. Five of the castles contain this element - Dunvegan, Duntulm, Dun Sgathaich, Dun Ringill and Dunakin (Caisteal Maol). Though the word might also be applied to a hill or fortified mound it is invariably used to describe a prehistoric broch or dun in the same way as 'caster' indicates the site of a Roman fort further south. That this very specific use of the term was both widely recognized and meticulously applied is indicated by the fact that the predecessors of Duntulm and Caisteal Camus were known as Dun Dhaibhidh and Dun Thorovaig.

The cumulative weight of topographic factors, tradition and occurrence of the 'dun' element in the name convincingly points to all but three of the ten castles occupying sites already of some antiquity when the mediaeval defences were raised. Under the circumstances it is perhaps not surprising to note that the three castle – Caisteal Uisdean, Brochel and Clachan known to have been of new foundation in the Middle Ages, contain none of the above characteristics.

Given the prehistoric antecedents of the castles, there arises the question as to what role these earlier works played in their genesis. It is claimed that some were the residences of Scandinavian chiefs; this is understandable given the need to explain what could only be understood in terms of what was known 'historically'. The belief that brochs and duns were 'Danish Forts' persisted into the 19th century and only then, were the structures shown to have been already over a thousand years old. There is one site within the district which perhaps holds the key to the fascinating relationship between prehistoric defences and mediaeval fortifications. Dun Ringill is a remarkably well preserved Iron Age broch-like structure, raised on a small projecting mass of rock overlooking Loch Slapin. In the Middle Ages it was reoccupied and

Birlinn carved on the tomb at Rodil, Harris, of *Alasdair Crotach* (died 1547) (from K. A. Steer & J. W. M. Bannerman, *Late Medieval Monumental Sculpture in the West Highlands*, HMSO, 1977).

substantially strengthened by the addition of lime-mortared walls to provide a fitting stronghold for the chief of Clan MacKinnon. This appears to have been the place referred to in the Act of Council of 1360 as Castle Findanus, and its uniquely revealing blend of Iron Age structure and mediaeval refurbishment doubtless owes its preservation to a decision to build a more suitable stronghold at Kyleakin in the later 14th or early 15th centuries. The revelation that similar structures might have been adapted as residences for the early clan chiefs would certainly explain the predilection for sites of earlier settlement. It would also help in explaining why the majority of recognizably mediaeval work appears to be stylistically late, given that the clan chiefdoms had already been resident here for some centuries. Indeed the MacAskills reputedly held Dun Sgathaich under Norse government and, by the late 13th century, the MacLeods were in residence at Dunvegan, possibly in succession to the MacRailds. Yet the only clear structural evidence for pre-14th century mediaeval works appears to have been the curtain wall at Dunvegan, and possibly the adaptations at Dun Ringill already referred to.

In the light of the large and imposing residences later constructed at many of these sites, there is a danger of underestimating the complexity of the earlier works and their presence dominating the landscape. These structures existed in a mixed Scandinavian-Celtic realm that, until the middle of the 13th century, formed part of the possessions of the King of Norway. This world had little in common with Norman feudalism which had been penetrating the Scottish kingdom since the early 12th century, and consequently the early castle forms which reflect feudal order – such as the motte and bailey – do not appear here. Even when these territories were ceded to the Scottish crown by the Treaty of Perth in 1266, the immediate beneficiary was not the Crown but the Lord of the Isles. This Lordship retained a high regard for the Gaelic language, culture and customs, and the Crown's long struggle to impose a proper feudal superiority over this remote north-western territory was to take a further 250 years to achieve.

While the difficulties in reconciling a feudal order with long-established practices continued to erupt periodically into open conflict between the Crown and its subjects in the West, these island chiefs proved less resistant to the influences of castle construction elsewhere. Probably in the 13th century, the enceinte, a substantial enclosure

containing and protecting the buildings within, was built under Leod or his successor, Norman, at Dunvegan. The enclosing wall at Dun Sgathaich might well date to the same period which, together with the mortared work at Dun Ringill, represents the earliest use of lime-mortared construction in the district.

During the 13th century the popular form of castle layout involved placing a substantial *donjon* or tower at the rear of the enclosure. The impracticalities of this arrangement were soon revealed, and subsequently remedied by building large gate-towers over the gateway which had always been the weakest point in a castle's defences. Other than where the great fortresses were concerned, the older layout proved a popular one for more lightly fortified residences and particularly so in the Border lowlands. Usually these stood some four storeys in height with a parapet, and contained a great hall at first floor level with a basement below and private apartments above. It seems not uncommon for a garret to have been included within the roof and, of those built within the district, there seems to have been an excessive fondness for intra-mural passages and stairs that might owe much to familiarity with the brochs.

One of the first built within the district was the large tower at Dunvegan which appears to have been constructed in the 14th century. This was followed thereafter by similar ones at Eilean Donan, Caisteal Maol, Duntulm, Caisteal Camus (all later 14th or early 15th century), and, possibly, also at Dun Sgathaich. The latest in date was the stronghold built at Caisteal Uisdean shortly after 1600, by which time the island chiefs were turning towards other and more comfortable forms of construction.

Where the area available permitted, a curtain-wall with a parapet walk and gateway enclosed both the tower and a courtyard area. Within this would have stood the subsidiary buildings necessary to the functioning of a household, such as stores for food, fuel and household goods, stables, sheds and perhaps accommodation for retainers and visitors. Dun Sgathaich, Duntulm, Eilean Donan, Caisteal Camus and Dunvegan have courtyards encircled by curtain-walls with towers at some, or all, of the angles. Courtyard wells are recorded for Brochel, Dunvegan and Dun Sgathaich, and it is not unreasonable to assume that there were wells at the others also.

The construction of such solid buildings was clearly a laborious undertaking, and their repair and maintenance thereafter would

Silver brooch of the late 14th or early 15th century found at Waternish, North Skye, in the 19th century. It measures only 27mm. in diameter (National Museums Scotland).

require skilled craftsmen. These, together with a large body of labourers, would be engaged for some time in quarrying and dressing stone, trimming the timbers, preparing vast quantities of shell-lime mortar required to bond the walls, erecting scaffolding, covering roofs with slate, thatch or lead, and providing drainage. As many of the materials would not be readily to hand much would need to be transported over some distance. Conveying them by land was virtually out of the question in a daunting landscape treacherous enough to a traveller on foot or horseback. Transport by sea offered a far easier means of carriage, reaffirming the soundness of choosing sites near to the shore.

Given that what natural woodland existed on Skye was almost wholly confined to the southern part of the island, most of the timber required for scaffolding, joists trusses, rafters and other components is likely to have been obtained there, from the mainland, or Europe. In all cases building stone, of variable quality, was available in the vicinity, although some effort was clearly expended in obtaining large quantities of lime-mortar to bond the masonry. While limestone of a quality suitable for hydraulic lime could be quarried near Broadford and on Raasay, preference seems to have been given to obtaining this from shells. Lime mortar was known as *lionn-tath*, and was poured into the core in its hot liquid condition.

With these materials, roughly coursed walls of hewn stone were raised. In most cases the angles appear to have been accorded no special treatment, and, at best, the stones used here were only marginally larger than those in the walls. Brochel is the exception, its substantial side-alternate quoining showing an uncharacteristic neatness at the angles.

It is unfortunate but not wholly surprising to find that the earliest

A bronze spur discovered in Loch St. Columba, Kilmuir, during drainage in 1824. Dating to the 12th century the spur measures 150mm. in length and is decorated with a pattern of interlacing ribbons enclosing quatrefoils. Originally it was gilded. There are nine sockets for semi-precious stones, five of which are filled (National Museums Scotland).

accounts relating to building works at a castle exist only for Dunvegan, and then no earlier than the 17th century. In 1623 Rory Mór, the 16th chief, paid £200 English for 5 ¼ tons of lead used to roof the building erected between the tower and Fairy Tower. That the earlier buildings were thatched or covered with oak shingles can only be surmised, however in 1665 12,700 roofing slates were brought in. As to the relationship between a master mason and an island chief at this period, a contract survives between Donald Ross and John MacLeod so revealing as to be worth quoting:

> ... Lykeas the said Donald Rosse binds and obliessis him and his foir-saids to the said John MacLeod and his spouse not to leave and depart fra the said worke to no person or persons upon no pretence or cullor whatsoever. But to abyd thereat till the finall end & decision & finishing of the same and that under the pane of four score punds money foresaid &c. For the quhilkes premisses sua to be done by the said Donald Rosse the said Johne MacLeod binds and obleises him & his foirsaids ...

> ... to content & pay to the said Donald Ross and his foresaids the sum of tua hundreth & fourtie pounds Scottis money at the termes following ... Togidder also with ten balls meal, six balls malts, eight stanes butter, eight stanes cheese and sixteene wedders. To be payit to the said Donald whensoever the same shall be requyrit be him. Lykeas the said Johne Mac Lead not onlie binds and obleises him and his foirsaids to furnish to the said Donald Ross during his working at the said work four barrow men whensoever they shall be required be the said Donald Ross, but also to furnish all other materialls of stane, lyme, & scaffolding requisite for the said worke, And to put the same within the close of Dunvegan and that under the pane of four score pounds money fair-said. In case of failzie, etc. Donald MacLeod of Grisernish is a witness to the contract.
>
> (At Dunvegan 3 December 1664.)

Providing contractors with victuals such as malt, butter, or cheese was a practical way of disposing of surplus rents in kind rather than parting with hard cash. Currency does not seem to have been easy to come by, a fact Prince Charles Edward Stuart discovered when wishing to change a guinea at Portree before seeking haven on Raasay. The best the innkeeper could muster was 13 shillings. Similar difficulties were experienced by Dr. Johnson towards the end of the century, although he was able to remark that people on Skye were 'now acquainted with money'. Until the 16th century most of the lesser tenants would rarely have dealt in coin of the realm, discharging their rents rather by a system of payments in kind. In the 16th century a 'Penny-land' with an annual rental of £1 4s 2d Scots was paid with 6 stone of meal, 6 stone of cheese, 1 cow, and 4s 2d in cash; a 'farthing-land' was reckoned at only 3 stone of meal and 3 stone of cheese. Until well into the 17th century some rents in Skye continued to be paid partly in kind – usually meal, cheese, butter and cows. On Harris some rents were paid in linen, valued at 6s 8d per ell (42 inches), or with tweed valued at 8s. an ell.

Together with other feudal dues, such as the chief's right to the best cow or horse on the death of a tenant (*heriot*), the chief's household might thus be tolerably well maintained in a traditional manner. The various political entanglements of the 15th and 16th centuries, however, combined with the consuming passion for the luxurious lifestyle of the south, involved the chiefs in crippling debts. Hard cash, rather than produce was needed, and therefore an instrument was sought whereby this could be obtained without necessarily selling off the estates. By the 17th century it was becoming common practice for a chief to let out part of his estate on 'tack' to a middleman who would undertake to pay a fixed cash sum for the rental. While this also included part payment in kind, the chief now received a guaranteed income without having to deal directly with the lesser tenants, at the same time still retaining the rights of ownership. In addition a Tacksman was obliged to pay an entry fee together with an obligation to render military service.

No less appealing to a chief was the system of 'wadset' which had made its appearance by the beginning of the 16th century. This was a form of mortgage, the 'wadsetter' making a cash loan to the chief and receiving as security the rights to receive the income from lands until the debt had been repaid. The occupier was compelled to pay both Crown and ecclesiastical dues, although he might sub-let and sub-divide the lands to his own profit. In theory the 'wadsetter' was in the

Late mediaeval grave-slab on St. Columba's Island, Skeabost. The slab shows a kilted warrior within a niche, and with his feet resting upon a mediaeval birlinn (galley). In the post-mediaeval period a winged angel was carved in the top right-hand corner, and initials of MacSweens in the top left; presumably this was done when the stone was re-used to mark later burials.

more precarious position, for, unlike the Tacksman, the property could be reclaimed on repayment of the loan. In practice the chiefs found such debts not so easily discharged.

Closer to the chief were his retainers, and towards the end of the 14th century it was becoming increasingly common to find a local lord supporting large numbers of men, armed and liveried as tenants. Their purpose was to subdue opposition by intimidation and fight on his behalf in any quarrels. This abuse of the feudal order was particularly prevalent in England, where statutes against 'livery' passed as early as 1377, culminated in Henry VII's eventual suppression of this evil in 1504. That the problem also extended into Scotland is evident from the actions of the Scottish kings against overpowerful and ambitious earls. William, the 6th Earl of Douglas, kept such a band and:

'quhair evir he raid he was convoy it with an thousand horsman at sum tymes twa thousand or ma. Amangis quhome he maintenit a gret companye of thewis [thieves] and murthiraris [murderers] and would bring thame to Edinburghe or any vther townis of sett purpois in the Kingis sicht [sight] to lat him vnderstand his michtie power'.

A chess piece of mid-13th century date discovered in Loch St Columba, Kilmuir, during an attempt to drain the loch in 1763 (National Museums Scotland).

The growth of private mercenary armies was clearly unacceptable to Crown Authority, yet the measures imposed to combat this also affected what had been a long-standing practice of the chiefs in the west to maintain a retinue of personal bodyguards, selected for their prowess and fighting abilities. It was said that Donald Gorm MacDonald would have no man in his bodyguard who could not lift a *cogie* (wooden dish) holding enough gruel for twelve men with one hand. This was then passed with fingers outspread for the next to take. They were known as the *luch-taighe* (household troop) or *Buannachan*, indicating that their residence was usually within the castle. By an Act of Council of 1616 the numbers of such men that the island chiefs might keep was limited. MacLeod and MacDonald were restricted to keeping only 6 of each, while MacKinnon of Strath was allowed only 3. Formerly Donald Gorm MacDonald had 16 in his household and MacLeod had 12. That such a group was not always popular amongst the clansmen is illustrated by the story of Finlay of the White Plaid who lived in Glendale. He had occasion to disarm, tie up and return MacLeod's 12 bodyguards, delivering them up to the chief with stern words of disapproval on how they had abused their position in bullying the chief's people.

As to the other retainers that might be housed within a chief's residence, the Gaelic language furnishes a list of those appropriate to a chief's position:

| | |
|---|---|
| *Gille-graidh* | secretary or chiefservant. |
| *Fear-cogaidh* | fighting man. |
| *Fear-feachd* | guard or watchman. |
| *Gille-coise* | footman. |
| *Gille-ceann-each* | man who leads horses. |
| *Gille-comh-streathainn* | attendant for the chief's horse. |
| *Gille-each* | stable boy/groom. |
| *Gille-truis-airnis* | courier and carrier of chief's baggage or purse. |
| *Gille-cupa* | cup-bearer. |
| *Gille-cas-fluich* | man who, when required, carried the chief over rivers and in and out of boats. |

This patriarchal order had its own complex system of rewards. The chief's stewards for example were assigned a township and lands in return for their service. Even the division of an animal was according to custom; the armour-bearer received a double portion of meat, and the quartermaster had a claim on the hides.

In the later 17th century Martin Martin noted that the chiefs still retained standard-bearers, quartermasters and armour-bearers. He also reports that a lookout or 'cockman' was always at his post to give a warning of strangers, and it is known that this practice continued at Duntulm into the early 18th century, with a 'cockman' posted by a small cannon. At dinner the chief was attended by his steward whose duty it was to ensure that the seating positions of the guest reflected their rank and position. Guests were attended by a cup-bearer whose responsibilities also included drinking the first draught.

In a lyrical passage composed in 1678 by Ian Lom, lamenting the death of Sir James MacDonald of Duntulm, he furnished a glimpse of these servants at work:

Your servants in turn would be filling drink of the finest taste. They would have red Spanish wine and beer, whisky in

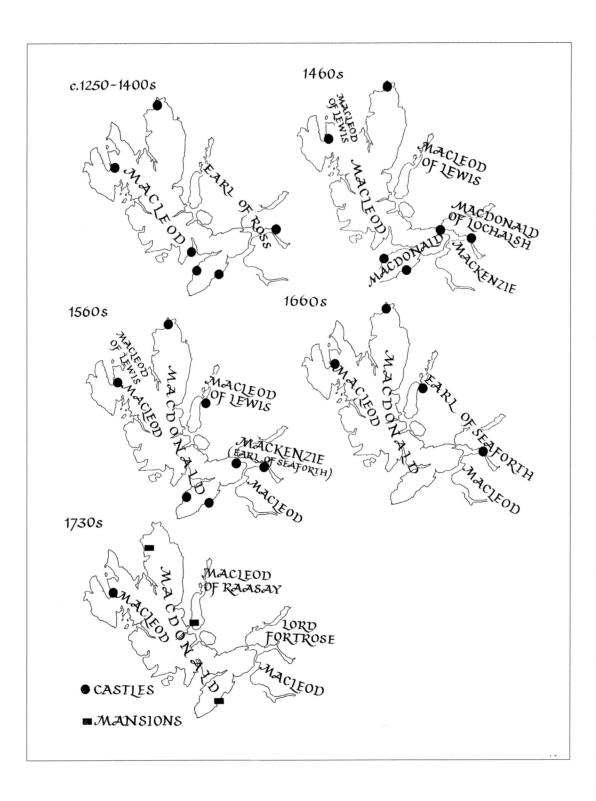

c.1250–1400s

1460s

MACLEOD
OF LEWIS

MACLEOD

EARL OF ROSS

MACLEOD
OF LEWIS

MACLEOD

MACDONALD
OF LOCHALSH

MACDONALD

MACKENZIE

1560s

1660s

MACLEOD
OF LEWIS

MACLEOD
OF LEWIS

MACDONALD

MACKENZIE
(EARL OF SEAFORTH)

MACLEOD

MACDONALD

EARL OF SEAFORTH

MACLEOD

1730s

MACLEOD
OF RAASAY

MACDONALD

MACLEOD

LORD
FORTROSE

MACLEOD

● CASTLES

■ MANSIONS

their vessels. Money would go to buy it, and one would find it in the glass like a bead of gold.

Occasionally however, the meal could end less poetically in a 'rant' of drinking. Martin describes how a gathering would continue drinking, 'sometimes twenty-four, sometimes forty-eight hours; it was reckoned a piece of manhood to drink until they became drunk, and there were two men with a barrow attending punctually on such occasions. They stood at the door until some became drunk, and they carried them upon the barrow to bed, and returned again to their post as long as any continued fresh, and so carried off the whole company one by one as they became drunk'.

Until the later 17th century the Government kept a wary eye on these remote Island strongholds. A covert survey of their strength was commissioned sometime between 1577 and 1595, and during the troubled year of 1689 a troop of Government horse was imposed on Dunvegan to discourage local restlessness from erupting into outright rebellion. By this time however, the world out of which the old strongholds had grown was passing. Though in the early 18th century Duntulm could boast cannon, at Dunvegan the role of these weapons had already been reduced to that of dummies in stone. Structures suitable only for military activity on a limited scale had long been unequal to the large armies and new technology which a powerful central authority could deploy against them. When the flourish of a royal pen in London could determine the ownership of a remote castle in the Isles, a chief's security depended far more on political acumen than high towers and stout walls. Their world was giving way to a new

*Opposite.* The shifting pattern of tenure by the main clans between the 13th and early 18th centuries. Between any pair of maps several changes could and, indeed, did take place. Also the maps do not necessarily reveal the Feudal Superior. Castles are marked where known to have been in occupation at these dates.

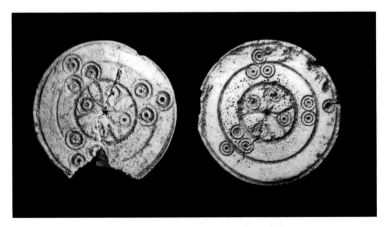

Two bone gaming-pieces, ornamented with dots and circles, found at *Eilean Donan* Castle. Diameter 48mm. (National Museums Scotland).

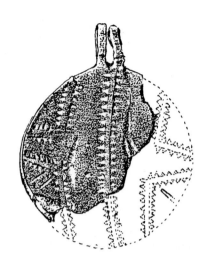

A 14th-century bronze mirror-case found in a circular stone building at Tungadal, Bracadale, Skye. It measures only 28mm. in diameter and was opened like a powder-compact to reveal a small glass backed by lead foil. Probably made on the continent or in London, this is the most northerly example known. Its upper face is decorated with close-set punched triangles (Dualchas, drawn by Marion Roberts).

order, a fact that the Island chiefs were made well aware of during their increasingly frequent journeys to the south. By the terms of the Statutes of Iona as revised in 1616, and to which the Island chiefs were compelled to agree, King James VI imposed great restraints on Highland life. Though many of the enactments were disregarded by the chiefs, the requirement that the children of a chief be educated in the lowlands and learn English was certainly followed. Rory Mór's library at Dunvegan could boast amongst others, the works of Hippocrates, Homer, Boethius, Euclid, together with various Greek lexicons, and doubtless those of the other clan heads were no less well furnished.

During the course of the 17th century the steady penetration of southern influence into the fabric of Highland life was both permanent and profound. This was neither a new nor a sudden event, but part of a more prolonged process of change begun a century earlier, and arising from the replacement of the regional authority of the Lordship of the Isles by the direct authority of a State able to hold its own in a Europe then exploring both itself and the wider world. The transformation that took place over the following two centuries in the relationship between a chief and his kin would ultimately turn chiefs into landlords and kinsmen into crofters (see R. A. Dodgshon, *From Clan Chiefs to Landlords*, Edinburgh University Press. 1998). It was, however, one evident at a variety of lesser levels, not least in modes of dress. Amidst the often quirky observations of a late 17th-century native of Skye, it was noted that older fashions had been abandoned and now 'persons of distinction wear the garb in fashion in the South of England'. The 17th century household accounts for Dunvegan bear ample testimony to this trend in extensive lists of imported materials for elegant dress – London cloth, English stockings, silks, taffeta, velvet and lace sewn together with gold and silver threads and sporting elaborately decorated buttons of gold and silver.

Many household items which an earlier age might have expected to have been produced within the district were now being purchased abroad. Sadly, not a single piece of the earlier mediaeval furniture has survived from any one of the chiefly residences, all being replaced at the dictate of comfort and fashion by imported goods. The large and elaborately decorated sideboard forming one of Dunvegan's treasures is plainly not from the hand of an inspired Celtic craftsman, but reputedly the product of a London workshop in 1603, brought to the castle by Rory Mór in 1619. The household accounts also catalogue an array of other imports such as chairs, kettles, glasses, locks, plates and trenchers, and an oven.

Framed portraits or religious paintings now hung on walls formerly decorated only with hangings and trophies. Indeed Sir Donald MacDonald engaged someone to teach his wife Mary the art of 'limning' (painting) on glass at Duntulm in 1704–6, as well as lessons on the *viol da gamba*. The catalogue of new imports is remarkable, including castanets for Mary MacDonald. Amidst the claymores and targes at Dunvegan, now stood fishing rods and golf clubs, testimony to the gentlemanly skills now required.

On a larger scale this change of manners found expression in the buildings themselves. A changing political situation, the military inappropriateness of the large tower residences, and the steady permeation of the Southern influences converged to stimulate what in the 18th and 19th centuries would develop into the imposing mansions of the clan chiefs. By the early 17th century this trend was in motion with the construction of a new style of building within the castle enceinte, influenced by the rural mansions or rectangular buildings at that time being constructed in the towns. Remains of these are plain at Duntulm, Caisteal Camus, Dunvegan and Dun Sgathaich, and except for Dunvegan, appear to represent a final major building phase. These rectangular halls are remarkably uniform in size, with a ground-plan proportion of 2:1 ranging from 18m. x 9m. at Dunvegan to 10m. x 4.5m. at Duntulm. Evidence indicates that they appear to have shared something of the earlier fashion for height. That at Dunvegan, built in

Detail from a later mediaeval illustration showing an early handgun in use during a siege.

1623, contained three floors and a garret. Those raised at Duntulm and Caisteal Camus consisted of two floors, probably with garrets in the roof space. In place of narrow loops admitting only a trickle of light into the older buildings, the availability and relative cheapness of window glass allowed for larger window openings, now piercing thinner walls.

Where the castle area available for new buildings was restricted, new residences were built elsewhere. In the opening decades of the 17th century Caisteal Maol was abandoned for a new chief's residence at Kilmarie, and nearer the original seat of the clan. By its close the MacLeods of Raasay had deserted Brochel Castle for Clachan, where the new house was burnt down by Government troops after the 1745 Rebellion. Fire also destroyed the residence near Armadale built by the MacDonalds of Duntulm. By this time the limitations of dwelling places determined by now-outmoded needs for defence were being felt acutely. With the sole exception of Dunvegan, by the early decades of the 18th century the castles which had controlled and nurtured the spirit of clan society for over six centuries lay abandoned and desolate. Relics of an age which was passing into obscurity were thereafter only valuable to be picked over for building materials, a subject for antiquarian curiosity or a plaything of the elements.

## ACCESS TO THE CASTLES

With the exception of Eilean Donan and Dunvegan where visitors are welcomed during a large part of the year, access to many of the castles invariably involves crossing land in crofting and private ownership. Whilst a route to each castle is given, this does not convey permission to visit a site without prior agreement of the owner. Wherever possible this should be sought before visiting a castle, and, please, close any gates behind you on the route. Dogs are not welcome on most sites.

# Brochel Castle

NG 5846 4627

PORTREE PARISH

## ROUTE

Follow the road northwards up the west side of Raasay and across to the east where it sweeps down above the castle. Park here and cross the fence by the stile, dropping down the slope. The castle is fenced as a dangerous structure and the stonework is so insecure that access is to be discouraged until such time as the building has been made safe.

Detail from William Daniell's aquatint of Brochel Castle seen from the north-west. In 1819, when this view was made, the north-eastern tower was standing behind the 'keel-shaped' north-western tower. The figure is standing on the south-west, kitchen, tower.

Impossibly fantastical illustration of Brochel Castle by the 19th-century artist Horatio McCulloch.

## HISTORY

The island of Raasay, together with the islands of Rona, Fladday and Eilean Tigh to the north, probably formed part of the possessions of the MacLeods of Lewis, or Siol Thorcuil as they were known. Throughout the 14th and 15th centuries these latter islands had become the refuge of 'thieves, ruggers [robbers] and reivairs', disrupting by their piracy the sea-borne traffic across the Inner Sound. At the turn of the 16th century, Calum MacLeod, the 9th Chief of

Lewis bestowed the lands of Raasay and Rona on his younger son, Calum Garbh. Thereafter known as MacGillichaluim, Calum became the first chief of the Raasay MacLeods albeit 'the weakest and least powerful of all the island Lairds'.

The documentary sources are silent as to when the castle at Brochel was built. The style of the building suggests construction in the 15th century. Although tradition records that it belonged to the MacSweens, possession by the first laird of Raasay, Calum MacGillich-aluim, before 1518 might seem a more appropriate occasion for its construction. Tradition, however, is clearer as to the origins of the castle. Though failing to supply a date for the construction it gives in fulsome measure the circumstances by which the money to build it was obtained.

Once upon a time, so the story goes, a MacLeod of Raasay was out hunting on Glamaig with his *Gille-Mor* or henchman. After a fruitless day they returned to their boat only to discover that a favourite hunting dog was missing. They whistled for it without luck and the Gille-Mor was for returning to find it but the chief said that if they returned in the morning it would probably be waiting on the shore. On returning in the morning and after a long search there was still no sign of the dog. Having given up the search they were sailing back across the loch when they imagined they could hear a dog barking in the neighbourhood of Loch Sligachan. Setting the prow in that direction they discovered a large birlinn at anchor there, with the missing dog on board. The Gille-Mor leapt aboard to retrieve it but was seized by the crew who attempted to throw him back over the side. They had sorely miscalculated the Gille-Mor's strength, for soon it was they who went overboard. Seeing the turn things were taking, a youth on board grabbed the dog and tried to get below decks, however he was seized by the Gille-Mor and flung aside. The dog was retrieved and on return it was revealed that the birlinn belonged to the Laird of Craignish and that the youth on board, his son, had been mortally injured.

Some time after, at a great gathering of chiefs at Dunvegan. MacLeod of Raasay was talking to the Laird of Craignish after supper when Craignish pulled a purse of gold from his pocket and promised it to anyone who would tell him who had killed his son. MacLeod's Gille-Mor, who was in attendance on his chief, asked him if he really meant that. On receiving an assurance he held out his hand for the gold which he put in his sporran. 'I am sorry to say it was I,' said the *Gille-Mor*, 'but it was his own fault and an accident, for which I am grieved.' He waited to see what would happen, but nothing did. Finally he held out his hand, which Craignish took, then bowed and left the room. He was soon followed by his chief, who felt it was prudent that they leave for home quickly. Some days later the Gille-Mor came to his chief and pressed the gold on him, saying he neither had a need for it, nor would his conscience allow him to keep it. MacGillichaluim took the money and used it to build Brochel Castle.

The castle is first mentioned by Dean Monro in 1549, as being one of 'twa castellis' on the island. Like its neighbour at Clachan, Brochel possessed a 'fair orcheart' (not necessarily an orchard in the modern sense but perhaps a garden).

This was presumably situated on the more level ground to the south. In the military survey undertaken between 1577 and 1595 the daunting position of the fortress impressed the compilers to record, 'ane strong little castell in this ile, biggit on the heid of ane heich craig, and is callit Prokill'.

The last chief resident at Brochel is reputed to have been Iain Garbh (Mighty John), a man of prodigious strength who succeeded his father Alexander in 1648. He was greatly venerated by his tenants, and with his death it seems that there was a vacuum in the succession until his cousin Alexander became the 8th Chief in 1692. Thereafter, if not before, the chief residence was at *Clachan*.


DESCRIPTION


That anyone could have conceived of building a castle on this bare monumental stack of Torridonian sandstone reveals powerful ingenuity at work. That it could be so built as to integrate every irregularity and draw the uneven stepped plateau together into the one formidable complex, is a triumph of design and execution.

Today the castle presents a distressing aspect of neglect and apparent unconcern at the demise of this, perhaps one of the most picturesque of all the castles in the district. Great upstands of walling now hang precariously, their footings undercut and their lime-mortar eaten away by the elements. All around the base of the stack lies the evidence of former collapse. Yet, until relatively recently, the walls were

In 1841 Brochel Castle was sketched by Sir Thomas Dick Lauder. In this, the only view from the north-east, drum-towers are shown on the south-east (lower) tower. These are figments of the imagination.

standing intact, and the castle's arrangement plainly visible to 18th century visitors.

It was doubtless this 'very whimsical and picturesque structure', combined with the visual drama of its setting, which compelled William Daniell to draw the castle for an engraving in 1819. This preserves a great deal of evidence for the superstructure, and reveals just how much architectural detail and embellishment has since been lost. On the basis of his work far greater sense can be made of what remains.

Just 46 years earlier the site was visited by Dr. Johnson and James Boswell and the remarks of the latter are so revealing as to be worth quoting:

> The old castle is situated upon a rock very near the sea.
>
> The rock is not one mass of stone, but a concretion of pebbles and earth; but so firm that it does not appear to have mouldered. I perceived no pieces of it fallen off. The entry was by a steep stair from the quarter next the sea, of which stair only three or four steps are remaining, all at the top of it. Above them the castle projects, and there is an opening in the wall from which hot water or stones could be thrown

upon an invader. Upon entering the gate or door, there was what I never saw before: a sentry box or alcove in the wall on your right hand. The man placed there could only watch in case of noise. He could see nothing. The next advance was to a court or close as it was called, in the centre of four towers, and open above just like any other court of an old castle in the square form. Only that this seemed extraordinary, as you came to it after ascending a stair and entering a gate; but as Mr Johnson observed, it was just an ordinary court, with the difference that the rock here was as the ground in others. The court here was very small. There was a fine well just a spring in the rock but it was now filled up with rubbish. One could distinguish tolerably that there has been four towers, but time and storms had left little but ruinous fragments: pieces of wall, pieces of stairs, a part of the battlement to the sea.

There was one small room in one of the towers quite entire. It was a little confined triangular place, vaulted as in the ancient manner. In a corner of it was a square freestone in which was cut an exact circular opening such as is in every temple of *Cloacina*, and from it there appears a clear communication to the bottom, that is to say anything will be carried by the outside of the rock to the bottom. They call this room the nursery, and say the hole was for the children. But I take it to have been the necessary-house of the castle. It was much to find such a convenience in an old tower. I did not imagine that the invention has been introduced into Scotland till in very modern days, from our connexion with England. But it seems we have forgotten something of civilized life that our ancestors knew.

(*The Journal of a Tour to the Hebrides with Samuel Johnson*, 1936 edn)

Boswell's 'Temple of Cloacina' is, as he correctly adduces, the 'necessary-house of the castle'. It is the garderobe or toilet. (From '*cluo*' Latin, 'I cleanse' – a sewer or drain. (It is also the surname of Venus, whose image stood where the Romans purified themselves with myrtle boughs after the Sabine War.)

The complex is comprised of four discrete 'apartments' – the four towers observed by Boswell. Each one linked by short stretches of curtain wall or the rockface itself, with access on the eastern coastal side through a deep gate-house passage. The entrance is approached by a ridge so narrow and steeply angled as to have prohibited wheeled traffic.

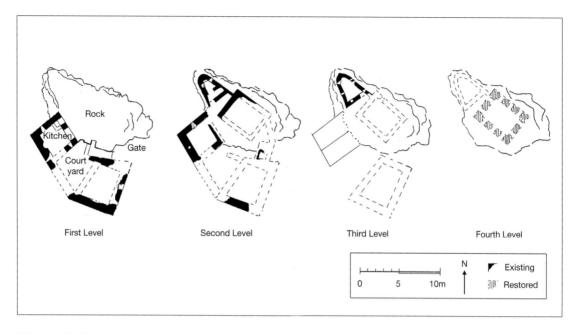

First Level

Second Level

Third Level

Fourth Level

0     5     10m

N

Existing

Restored

## THE GATE-HOUSE

Plan of Brochel Castle by levels (based upon RCAHMS).

The approach to the main entrance is by a narrow passage formed by an eastward projection of the castle on both sides of a narrow cleft in the rock. Under the shadow of such 'outworks' any assault on the castle would have posed the daunting prospect of being assailed from above on three sides. No traces now remain of the projection over the entrance noted by Boswell, with its opening 'from which hot water or stones could be thrown upon an invader'. An opening is, however, visible high up in the wall of the tower to the south, doubtless positioned to add to the protection of the gate.

The gate entrance has now fallen away in a cascade down the ridge, taking with it all evidence for the door-checks and bar holes which would have secured the stout wooden door. Within is a long narrow passage roofed with slabs and rising steeply by means of the steps. This passes beneath the gate-house. The south wall of this passage also forms the north wall of a tower lying to the south. The north wall however is just a facing against the natural bedrock which rises up to a plateau at a higher level. Near the top of the stairs there is a deep recess into the bedrock on the right-hand side. Its side walls are formed of coursed stone, and covered by a thin slab lintel, and this is, without doubt, Boswell's 'sentry box'. The purpose of the small platform in the corner angle beyond is unclear, neither is it clear what use was made of the small stone-shelved recesses in the wall facing the stair. It is, however, worth noting the small window above, permitting those inside the south-west tower to observe who was entering the castle.

## THE COURTYARD

The top of the stairs opens out onto a small open courtyard flanked to east and west by high towers. With the bedrock rising to the north, and the curtain wall forming the southern boundary, the courtyard must have presented a claustrophobic and cheerless aspect on all but the sunniest of days. Boswell remarked upon a well in this courtyard, now hidden beneath fallen masonry and debris.

## THE SOUTH-EASTERN TOWER

The tower to the east of the courtyard is a trapezium, widening to the south and enclosing an area of some 14 square metres. The east and south walls are nearly a metre in thickness, with a lime-mortar bonded core; the west wall is now reduced to a small linear mound. Presumably there was a doorway through this wall allowing access from the courtyard, and leading into a chamber lit by a window or windows in the east wall. Part of the internal splay forming the southern jamb of the southernmost window is still visible at the south-east corner of the room. There were no windows in the south wall at this level, but the wall survives to a height which suggests there once existed a second level above. This would indeed explain how access was gained to the chamber over the gateway, and bear out the early description of 'towers'. A view of the castle based upon a drawing made by Sir Thomas Dick Lauder in 1841 shows rounded towers rising above the wall-head level at either end of the east wall. Its tourelles existed only as a piece of artistic licence; photographs of the southern corner taken early in the present century and before it collapsed entirely clearly show only a plain angle formed of quoinstones.

Remnants of the corbel table carrying a projecting battlement remain on the outside, indicating that, as with the north towers, the roof was surrounded by a parapet.

## THE SOUTH-WESTERN TOWER

The principal entrance to this tower lay in the wall forming the west side of the courtyard. Its floor is now hidden beneath at least a metre depth of rubble. Traces of the seating for the joists of its ceiling are just discernible below and to the left of the window of the west wall. In the centre of the south wall is a fireplace, its circular flue rising up within the thickness of the wall. Presumably this was the kitchen, and the stone 'cupboards' recessed into the north wall intended for storing foodstuffs. Less clear, however, is the purpose of the small chamber in the corner to the west. This seems to have been a water tank for the run-off from the level above. There is a small window in the wall to the east of the fireplace.

The first-floor level above the kitchen was of identical floor area to that below – 7.5 square metres, with access to the plateau to the north by means of a steep flight of steps. One window remains: a much modified small light in the west wall which was originally larger, subsequently narrowed with fragments taken from elsewhere. Above this rose a gabled roof, plainly visible in Daniell's illustration. Daniell also illustrates a window at a level much lower than the kitchen floor and careful scrutiny of the exterior face today shows that a chamber at a lower level might well exist within this tower.

The castle from the west showing the two levels of the stepped plateau. The south-west, kitchen, tower occupies the lower plateau on the right.

### THE NORTH-EASTERN TOWER

This tower sits on the highest plateau to the north of the buildings described. Present access is only by scrambling up the walls from the kitchen, thereafter climbing the remains of a steep stone stairway. It is conceivable that another approach may have existed from the top of the gate-house.

The north-eastern tower survives only as an outline on the ground, although in 1819 it obviously stood pretty well entire. In his engraving Daniell shows it to have been rectangular and three storeys in height. There were no windows in the north and west walls at ground floor level, however a window is clearly shown in the north wall of the second floor. The roof was flat, with rain-spouts and crenellations carried by a corbel table.

### THE NORTH-WESTERN TOWER

This is the most complete of the castle's four towers, a small keeled structure also perched on the point of the very highest plateau. It was linked to both the north-eastern and south-western towers by short stretches of curtain wall which have now fallen away entirely. The ground floor is entered by a door at the south end of the east wall, opening into a narrow room. A door in the opposite wall leads into a still-smaller room, narrowing considerably where the stout curve of the north-east and south-west walls meet. At this point are two large 'cupboard' recesses of the kind already encountered, surmounted by a smaller recess. To the south-east of these is a larger recess of quite different purpose, the basal opening and chute projecting from the stonework below clearly indicating the garderobe or privy, referred to with 18th-century delicacy by Boswell as the 'temple of *Cloacina*'. This room is lit by a single small splayed light in the north-east wall. Both rooms were covered by a timber ceiling, the joist-holes for which are still plainly visible.

Access to the room above was through a door at the north end of the east wall, approached from a steep passage separating the two northern towers. A window, now blocked, lay to the right of the entrance with other windows set further along this wall, and another in the south-west wall above the garderobe. Other recesses are visible,

notably those high in the wall above the ground-floor entrance and smaller openings through the thickness of the adjoining walls. The latter may have been for drainage, and indicates a second floor above forming the flat roof of this tower. This is borne out by Daniell's illustration, where a projecting string course appears to carry a low parapet around the tower. The presence of a flat roof here is underlined by the absence of masonry chases on the adjacent tower into which lead soakers of a pitched roof would be mortared.

The entrance passage leading to the courtyard. Boswell's 'sentry-box' is set into the wall.

# Caisteal Camus

NO 6714 0870

SLEAT PARISH

ROUTE

Take the A851 Ardvasar road from Broadford, and continue past Isle Ornsay and the minor road to Ord and Tokavaig. Two kilometres beyond the Toravaig House Hotel there is a minor track on the left hand side of the road. Park here and walk past the farm steading to the entrance of the farmhouse. Here the track bears to the left and crossing a small bridge continues to a field gate and a small wicket gate in the fence. Go through the small gate, following the footpath past the stream and a boat-house before a short gentle ascent to the castle ruins.

*Caisteal Camus* from the west, showing the remains of the tower to the rear and right of the later building in the centre foreground.

## HISTORY

With the possible exception of a small ditch cut across the neck of the promontory, no trace now remains of the presumably Iron Age fort known as Dun Thoravaig ('The Dun of the Bay of Thor') that formerly occupied the site. The mediaeval castle raised over the earlier remains is first mentioned as the place where William, 4th Chief of the MacLeods, died in 1402. His heir, later known as Iain Barb (John the Truculent), was at the time only 10 years of age, and a Tutor or regent was required to act on his behalf until he attained his majority. The chosen Tutor proved a disaster. Iain Mishealbhach (John the Ill-fated) was indeed aptly named. Through his mismanagement the tightly knit pyramid which underpinned the chiefdom rapidly splintered into the restless and quarrelsome factions that arise whenever uncertainty and opportunism mingle. For MacDonalds settled outwith Skye the opportunities presented by discord within the Clan MacLeod proved irresistible. A host of MacDonalds invaded Sleat and with surprising ease Caisteal Camus and the MacAskill stronghold of Dun Sgathaich fell to their assaults. Encouraged by their successes the host determined

The southern angle of the tower with its only surviving window opening and largely missing wall-face. Centre and left is the south-facing frontage of the latest building on the site.

The eastern wall of the tower at the south-eastern end of the promontory.

to march on Dunvegan itself, but here their luck deserted them. On the journey northwards they were met by a large MacLeod gathering, whereupon the raiding band was decisively repulsed. Once again the MacLeods 'resumed tenure of the southern part of the island and presumably reoccupied Caisteal Camus after undertaking whatever repairs were required to make the castle once again habitable.

The following decades were critical to the future of the island. The events taking place at this time shaped the composition of the clan factions on Skye, around which its subsequent history over the following centuries was to revolve. In the earlier half of the 15th century Sleat formed part of the fiefdom of the Earl of Ross. It was as vassals of the Earl that the MacLeods owed their tenure in South Skye, although elsewhere the MacLeods held extensive territories by royal charter, such as that of Glenelg on the mainland opposite. Yet at this time the Earldom of Ross was poised on the brink of a crisis in the succession when Euphemia, Countess of Ross, who had succeeded to the Earldom, retired to a nunnery. Fortune had favoured Donald MacDonald, placing him through marriage in a position to lay claim to the title of Earl of Ross. Such an aggrandisment of power was seen as a threat by the Crown, and while subsequent events were to deprive Donald of legitimate title to the Earldom, it was accorded to his son Alexander of Islay, and grandson John. This transfer of territories into the hands of the Lordship of the Isles paved the way towards a MacDonald presence in the island. In 1463, John, Lord of the Isles, granted 28 merklands of territory in Skye to his brother, Celestine, and, just six years later, this was transferred to their third brother, Hugh. The grants were duly confirmed by royal charter in 1469 when Hugh of Sleat, as he came to be known, took up residence at Dun Sgathaich.

The MacLeods can hardly have been enthusiastic over their new

The castle astride its promontory, viewed from the east, and with the Sleat peninsula in the background. To the right of the castle, the line of the ditch is faintly discernible.

neighbours, especially considering their own removal to make way for them. However, as vassals of an Earldom now combined with the Lordship there was really little alternative. It is uncertain what effect this had on Caisteal Camus, however the local feeling is reflected in a story of how the MacDonalds drove out all the MacLeod men, but not the women. One day a MacDonald slipped above a treacherous drop and only saved himself by grasping a grass sod. A MacLeod woman was passing and, hearing his cries, came over to discover the terrified MacDonald's situation. 'Ah well, you've taken everything else, so I suppose you had better take this with you,' she said, and, with that, gave the sod a kick, sending it and the luckless MacDonald to the bottom.

In 1431 the castle had been overrun by royal troops during the struggles between James I and the Lordship, and for almost a century thereafter no mention is made of it. The castle does not resurface in the documentary records until 1513, when an attempt to resurrect the Lordship of the Isles was made in the person of Sir Donald Macdonald of Lochalsh, following the death of James IV at Flodden Field. In the uprising Alasdair Crotach MacLeod overran Dun Sgathaich and laid siege to Caisteal Camus. The situation for those besieged looked grave. Tradition relates that despite their hunger and privation a lady known to us only as 'Mary of the Castle' encouraged them to withstand the siege until Alasdair was compelled to acknowledge the hopelessness of the task and withdraw.

In 1549 Dean Monro recorded that the castle was, 'perteining to Donald Gromsome', however its most notable and longest established resident was James of the Castle. James was the fourth son of Donald Grumach, the 4th Chief of Sleat, and under his residency some considerable refurbishment might have been expected to take place. In his later years James was appointed co-regent with the brothers Hugh the Clerk and Donald for the young Donald Gorm Mor who had been left a minor of 6 or 7 years of age upon the death of his father, Donald Gormson. This regency was to prove the undoing of James, for in 1575 he signed a bond with his co-regents promising to pay the Bishop of the Isles the dues outstanding on the MacDonald lands. Reprimanded by the Crown in 1580 for non-payment, the following year the bond had still not been honoured and the co-regents were declared outlaws and their lands forfeit.

The reversion of these estates to the Crown offered the opportunity for new conditions to be imposed when it was regranted. Accordingly, when a new charter was given to Donald Gorm Mor in 1596 confirming him in the lands at Sleat, it contained the provision that in future Caisteal Camus was to be kept available as a residence for the King and his successors. Later this was reaffirmed in charters granted in July 1614 and August 1618, bearing witness as to how far royal influence in island matters had progressed since the first royal visit, by James V in 1540.

Could the large rectangular building representing the later phase of building at Caisteal Camus mark an attempt by the King to secure a royal residence on the Island? This spacious and apparently non-defensive dwelling appears to represent the last phase of major building work. Also, as it partially overlies the line of the west wall of the tower, it would seem to point to a period when the nascent tastes of a modern world were heralding the end of the mediaeval architectural tradition.

Sadly the King never used the residence he had been so keen to secure, and thereafter the demise of a fortification deprived of its *raison d'être* was swift indeed. The final documentary record which bears witness to occupation is in the form of a bond signed at the castle in August 1632, in which MacConillreich declared Sir Donald MacDonald, first Baronet of Sleat, to be his chief. By 1689 the building lay abandoned and desolate, useful only as a ready source of lintels and dressed stone with which to build the house of Knock and adjacent farm buildings during the course of the 18th century. So weakened was it by 1795 that the Reverend Martin MacPherson picturesquely delineates a sad ruin, 'partly ancient, partly modern, one side being circular and covered with ivy, the other being of the modern style of masonry' [the authors are quite bewildered by the use of the word 'circular'].

## DESCRIPTION

The castle sits on a bold headland overlooking the bay with spectacular views across the Sound of Sleat to the mainland opposite. The ground to the north rises in a gentle slope, westward of which the *Allt Gleann Thoravaig* winds its way southwards to debouch into a crook of the bay near the foot of the castle. To the south the steep near-vertical rock face gives an impregnable character to the towering ruins above.

## THE DITCH

Approached from the north, the remnant of a ditch flung across the neck of the promontory appears today only as a waterlogged hollow filled with reeds. Undoubtedly an element of the mediaeval defences, similar constructions to deter or delay assault appear around other Iron Age fortifications on Skye. The origins of this ditch might well lie with the earlier *dun* known to underlie the castle. Over the centuries depredation by the elements has been accelerated by stone-robbing, resulting in a confusion from which it is very difficult even to extract a ground plan of the buildings. In 1854 Horatio McCulloch executed a pencil and watercolour illustration of the castle, which both hints at its form as well as indicating the considerable deterioration which has taken place since this visit.

## THE TOWER

The oldest element now visible lies at the eastern end of the site, where a massive tower stood. Sturdy walls 1.5m. in thickness enclosed an area 18m. x 7m. containing at least three floor levels. Since the mid-19th century the south-west and north-west walls have been greatly reduced. They show today only as grass-covered linear mounds. Remarkably, the south-east wall still stands to a height of over 10m. At ground level there is a single window splayed internally, while from the outer face at the north end a garderobe debouches into the natural

'Knock Castle and the Sound of Sleat' 1854. This pencil, watercolour and bodycolour study of *Caisteal Camus* from the east was made as the basis for one of Horatio McCulloch's (1805–67) grand Highland scenes produced in the 1840s. Present whereabouts of the latter is unknown (McManus Galleries and Museum).

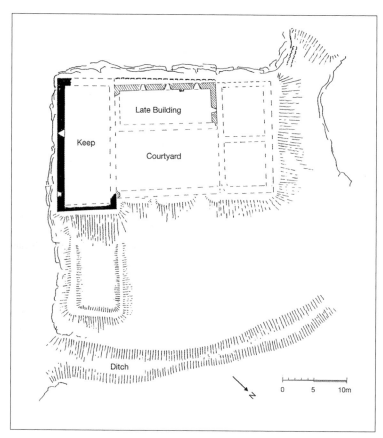

Plan of *Caisteal Camus.*

cleft in the rock. Only from this point is it possible to appreciate the skill with which the builders have melded outcropping rock and masonry. Every protrusion, cleft and undulation has been deftly knitted into an interlocking mesh of stonework to carry massive walls that rise as if out of the rock itself.

## THE CURTAIN WALL AND SOUTH-WESTERN BUILDING

The tower appears to have been entered from a courtyard to the south-west. A curtain wall running along the cliff edge linked it to a building at the south-west angle. Both the wall and building are now recognisable only by slight traces of their footings lying outside the frontage of more recent rebuilding on a slightly different alignment. This earlier building had disappeared even by the time McCulloch

The south-west wall from the interior of the late building at *Caisteal Camus*. The position of the former window openings is clear, as is the seating for the joists of the first floor level. The position of the hearth and chimney tunnel is seen to the right of the openings.

painted his view of the castle from the opposite shore. Footings indicate a building some 17m. by 8m. with a virtually central party wall dividing it into two square rooms. The circuit of wall appears to have continued off the north-east corner of this wing, making a screen between it and the tower on the landward side. It is likely to have been pierced by an entrance of the simplest form because there is not the slightest hummock to betray the existence of a gate-house.

## THE LATER BUILDING

Between this vanished wing and the tower was a courtyard in which was built a small late 16th or early 17th century house of rectangular plan, 17m. by 7.5m. externally. Its masonry is of smaller pieces of rubble than are found in the earlier walling. It is 'pinned' with even smaller flakes in a way reminiscent of that to be seen in contemporary building at Unish House or Eilean Donan, phase 3. From what little survives, it seems to have consisted of a basement with a heavily beamed ceiling, lit by four surviving narrow loops, three on the seaward side and one offset in the western gable. From the siting of a small fragment of cross-wall, it may have been divided into two rooms, with the larger being next to the tower. On the floor above were two rooms. Only the outer walls to the south-west and north-west survive and there to a height of some 5.75m. The smaller parlour or chamber lit by a single window at the end nearest the tower was lightly partitioned from a larger parlour. This had two windows overlooking the sea and two in its gabled end looking over the site of the two-roomed building. Only one feature has survived robbing-out and the elements, a semi-circular hearth-back haunched in a way suggestive of an iron-barred hearth for coals is set between the seaward windows of the larger parlour. There is no trace left of a fireplace in the basement or in the smaller parlour of the first floor. From the height of the gabled end as seen in McCulloch's view, it seems there were roomy garrets above. However, the drawing seems to be suspect in the overgenerous depth given to the block when compared with that of the existing footings. McCulloch's rendering is capable of misinterpretation. His light and shade suggest an additional building in advance of the wall-line at this point, a sort of mirage in which the long vanished wing has reappeared to overhang a sheer drop. The window shown offset on the ground floor is patently that still visible in the shattered stump of the north-west gable end. Close analysis shows that his painting is in fact reconcilable with the extant remains described here, that of a flat-fronted house abutting, but set back from, the tower, with its gable end windows looking over a vacant site. The new house had been harled and variations in dampness and lighting made it appear to project forward of the line of the cliff-edge curtain.

EXTERNAL BUILDING

Sheer below the north-east face of the tower is the outline of a rectangular building some 16m. by 7.5m. perhaps contemporary with the last phase of occupation from the late 16th century. Its position outside the castle proper suggests that it may have been built as a stable, or oxhouse, and barn. One explanation of its curious siting may be that its outer walls were intended to buttress the south-east end of the tower and its supporting cliff, which have now collapsed into a scree of rubble over its site.

# Caisteal Maol

NG 7580 2634

STRATH PARISH

ROUTE

From the ferry landing follow the main road through the village. Just before the carpark on the right hand side of the road, turn left through the village green and across the bridge. Continue along to the road-end, continuing thereafter by foot along the track. This follows the bay and goes past the boat-house to the castle.

HISTORY

*Caisteal Maol* ('the bare castle') occupies one of the most strategically important positions in the island. With an extensive commanding outlook of the narrows which separate the island from the mainland it was ideally situated to keep watch on passing shipping. In the Middle Ages it was known as Dunakin after the King of Norway in whose

'Kyle Akin and Entrance to Lochalsh'. In this later 19th-century engraving Caisteal Maol stands as a desolate ruin on the headland.

territories it once lay. In 1263 anyone stationed here would have witnessed the great fleet of King Haakon making its way south to defend Scandinavian possessions on the western seaboard against the claims of the Scottish Crown. From the Point of Sleat the same observer might also have witnessed the broken remnants of this fleet fleeing northwards after suffering defeat by Alexander III at the Battle of Largs. With the passage of this shattered fleet went Norway's final hopes of retaining a foothold in Scotland and, by the Treaty of Perth in 1266, sovereignty of the Western Hebrides was ceded to the Scottish Crown. It was to take Scottish kingship a further two and a half centuries to secure finally what had been won at Largs, for it was the Lords of the Isles who were most successful in capitalising on the Scandinavian defeat in the short-term.

Tradition relates that the castle was built by a Norwegian princess called 'Saucy Mary', married to a MacKinnon chief. Her main income was said to have derived from tolls levied on vessels sailing through the Kyle. Only ships of her own native land were exempt. To ensure that all others paid their dues, she had a massive chain strung across the Kyle from the mainland and fastened to a rock near the shore beside Kyle House. It is said that when she died her remains were interred beneath the large cairn on the top of Beinn na Caillaich ('Mountain of the Old Woman') so that the winds from her native shores could pass over her final resting place. While the fabulous quality of such traditions might cause a raised eyebrow, the circumstances which made them credible to an earlier age are not so easily dismissed. Before the later mediaeval castle was built some early remains may have been visible around which the 'Saucy Mary' legend was fabricated.

Only rarely do the paths of written historical testimony and archaeological evidence intertwine with such precision as they appear to do in response to the question as to when, exactly, Caisteal Maol was built. We have already noted that for much of the mediaeval period, the traditional seat of the clan lay within the old Iron Age dun at Dun Ringill, in Strathaird, with the MacKinnons recorded as resident there in 1360 AD (page xvi–xvii). While it is always possible that the MacKinnons held two castles at the one time, it is unlikely in the case of so minor a clan, and reasonable, purely on the 'historical' evidence, to presume it to be a new foundation, erected in the later 14th or, more probably, sometime within the 15th century. During the restoration of the structure in 1989, the stump-end of a major floor joist 300mm.

*Caisteal Maol* from the south-east photographed by Duncan MacPherson in the 1920s (Copyright Mrs M. Hudson).

square was found embedded within the castle wall. It was removed and sent to Belfast University, where dendrochronological dating of the tree-rings was 'wiggle-matched' to radiocarbon dates obtained from charcoal from individual rings. Together they showed that the timber had been felled towards the close of the 15th century. While it remains possible that the timber represents the renewal of an earlier one, its size and accord with the historical evidence might rather suggest a late 15th- early 16th-century date for the construction of this new seat of the MacKinnon chiefs.

Because of their close connections with the Lordship of the Isles, the early history of the MacKinnons is largely absorbed within the fortunes of this Lordship until its power was eventually broken by James IV in 1493. On James' death at Flodden in 1513, a great meeting of the rebellious chiefs was held at 'Dunakin', where they resolved to raise Sir Donald MacDonald of Lochalsh to the dignity of Lord of the Isles. The attempt soon fizzled out because the chiefs found Sir Donald

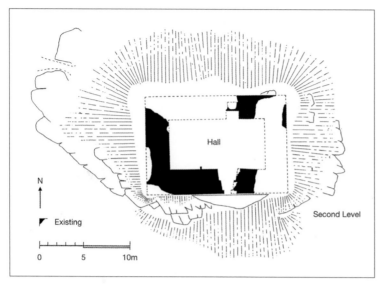

Plan of *Caisteal Maol*.

an unsuitable vehicle for their purposes and, by 1515, most of those involved in the conspiracy had received pardons from the Crown. The next reference to the castle is in 1549 when Donald Monro, High Dean of the Isles, noted 'the castill at DunnaKynne, pertaining to Mac-Kynnoun'. Dunakin, or the 'fort of Haakon' as it was known is an interesting name survival which reinforces belief in an earlier building on the site. This name appears on Timothy Pont's map of the island, drawn sometime around 1580. The castle is again mentioned in an account written between 1577 and 1595. Here it is called 'Dewnakin', and said to have been given to MacKinnon by one MacConneill in return for a judgement, 'betwin pairties threw playing at cairtis or dyce, or sic uther pastime'.

By then the days of MacKinnon residence were sadly numbered. The world had moved on and, with the emergence of strong central authority, families now sought to live out their lives in more comfortable and 'modern' surroundings. The final battle between the MacLeods and MacDonalds had taken place at Coire na Creiche in the heart of the Cuillin in 1601. In the fighting John Og, the younger brother of the 26th MacKinnon Chief was either killed or so badly wounded that he died young. His son Neill, progenitor of the MacKinnons of Kyle, was one of the last MacKinnons to reside in the castle, being brought up by his aunt Jane. (A relic from these times, a hoard of 70 coins, was discovered in 1951 hidden in a chink of masonry on the outer face of the west wall. Most of the coins were

In 1933 the Duke and Duchess of York visited Skye to open the new Boys' Hostel at Portree, They landed at Kyleakin and the castle is framed here as a backdrop to the Duchess' landing in a photograph taken by Duncan MacPherson (Copyright Mrs M. Hudson).

issued during the reign of James VI, and range in date from 1572 to 1601. Included in the hoard were two Scottish coins and an English coin of Mary, a James V issue, and an English sixpence of Elizabeth I.) By the early 17th century the seat of the MacKinnon Chief moved once more within its home territory when Kilmarie, not far from the original residence of Dun Ringill, was fixed upon as the family home. In 1616 and again in 1627, Lachlan MacKinnon held charters for his lands as a barony with rights for a ferry boat on the Kyle.

During the Civil Wars the MacKinnons supported the Royalist cause, and fought for the Marquis of Montrose at both Auldearn and Inverlochy in 1645. A MacKinnon regiment fought for Charles II at Worcester where the young chief was reputedly knighted by the King, although this was never confirmed. It was again as supporters of the Stuarts that the MacKinnons fought alongside the MacDonalds at Sheriffmuir in 1715, and at Glenshiel in 1719. While they were not present on the field at Culloden in 1746 they were operating in Ross and Sutherland on Charles Edward Stuart's behalf as part of Cromartie's force. Even when the cause was patently lost and the young Charles Stuart was a fugitive with a price of £30,000 on his

head, MacKinnon did not desert his Prince. Given shelter for a while in a cave to which Lady MacKinnon herself brought food and drink, he was eventually smuggled across the water to Loch Nevis. The old chief paid dearly for his actions, being seized and held in prison for two years longer than any others involved in the Rebellion. Tradition relates that it was from the Prince himself that the MacKinnons received the secret recipe for Drambuie liqueur. Sadly, within a generation the MacKinnon estate was broken up and sold to the MacDonalds of Sleat, with the district of Strathaird passing to the MacAlisters. By this time, however, the castle had lain abandoned for over a century. Desolate but not bereft of dignity the castle remains as a sentinel for those making passage across the narrows.

*The castle from the north in 1988.*

## DESCRIPTION

The castle occupies a small knoll of Torridonian sandstone to the east of Kyleakin. Time and the elements have not dealt kindly with the building. Of the once-substantial rectangular tower with mortar-bonded walls nearly 3m. in thickness, what remains now rather resembles some rotten primaeval tooth. In 1949 a large section of the western wall collapsed and, in the severe gales of February 1989, an equally substantial upstand on the north wall cascaded down the slope. As a result of this most recent damage the building was taken into care by Skye and Lochalsh District Council (subsequently subsumed within Highland Regional Council in 1996) with a view to its consolidation.

The castle is a simple rectangle in form with no indications of outworks. Its walls enclose an area 10m. east–west by 5m. north–south, all the space within being accommodation on three floor levels with possibly a fourth in the roof. Some indications of the various levels is preserved in the only substantial section of walling now surviving, that lying to the south which stands to a height of 12m.

The remains of the castle following the severe gales of February 1989, which brought down a section of the wall at the north-east corner.

## BASEMENT LEVEL

The lowest level is a large basement room, apparently without windows and entered only from first floor level. The ceiling was not vaulted, but consisted of timber joists seated on corbels like those by the window in the south-east wall. Opposite this window lie the remains of what may have been a garderobe or privy.

## THE FIRST FLOOR

The entrance, like that at Caisteal Uisdean, stood at first-floor level, although its position is no longer clear. Presumably it was approached by a stairway set against the outer wall-face which could be thrown down in emergencies. During repairs it was hoped to find indications of its seating to show on which side the doorway stood; sadly, this was not revealed. This doorway is likely to have opened into the hall which had a fireplace and stairs leading up to accommodation on the floors above. This hall was certainly lit by substantial windows, of which one survives in the south wall. This window lies within a recess in the wall thickness, covered by an arched vaulting, and, though it was the only window in this wall, it presumably had its counterpart in one or more of the other walls.

## THE SECOND FLOOR

The floor above was carried on joists set into a line of sockets still partly visible on a level just above the window-head. Too little now remains of this level, and those above, to reveal anything of their features. However, from a photograph taken around the turn of the century when the south wall stood to a height greater than today, it is just possible to make out either a small second-floor window or gun-loop on a line with that below. This is otherwise the only known aperture in this wall at second-floor level. Gaps in the wall at floor level might indicate other window positions.

# Caisteal Uisdean

NG 3804 5824

SNIZORT PARISH

ROUTE

Follow the A856 Poriree–Uig road northwards and past the branch road to Dunvegan (A850). At 1.3 km north of the bridge across the Hinnisdal River there is a farm track to South Cuidrach on the left. Follow this down to the gate and park either here, or, with permission, at the gate beyond. The track by the farm steadings will bring you out at the castle.

HISTORY

Caisteal Uisdean (Hugh's Castle) stands today as a stark monument to one of the darker characters of an age of treachery and deception. Hugh, or Uisdean MacGillespuich Chleirich was the son of Archibald, also styled the Clerk, half-brother of Donald Gorm, 5th Chief of Sleat.

The castle from the south.

When Donald died in 1539 attempting to storm the castle of Eilean Donan his son was still a minor, and the role of 'Tutor' or guardian to the young chief was undertaken by Archibald. In 1545, however, this position was assumed by Archibald's brother, John Og, and it was later rumoured that John had murdered Archibald to advance his position and extend his influence over the young chief.

Exactly three decades later another minority arose in the House of Sleat, when Donald Gormson, the 6th Chief died, apparently of natural causes. Hugh appears to have anticipated being given sole Tutorial authority for the young Donald Gorm Mor, and was therefore resentful to discover that this was to be shared between himself, his brother Donald, and their uncle, James of the Castle. This resentment doubtless appeared justified to Hugh, when in 1580 a summons against the three was made on account of unpaid dues owing to the Bishopric of the Isles. Donald died before sentence was passed in 1581, declaring James and Hugh rebels and outlaws, forfeit of their holdings.

*Caisteal Uisdean.*
1. Isometric drawings of the basement and first-floor levels.
2. Lateral section through the north-west wall showing the entrance and stair.
3. Window loop as a defensive measure.

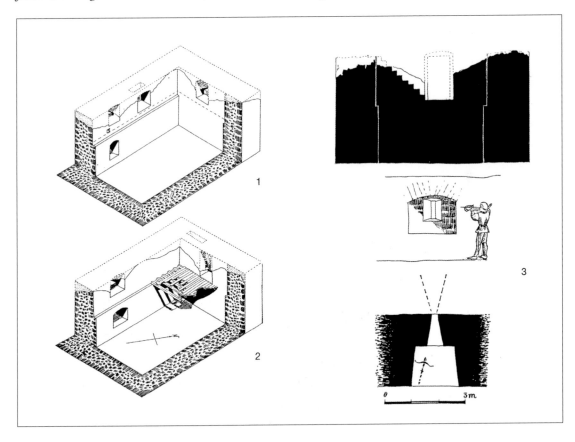

As the victim of an obligation entered into before he assumed Tutorial responsibility, no doubt Hugh believed himself to have been treated unfairly. Perhaps he also suspected his father to have been a casualty of devoted service to the chiefdom. In such situations most men bewail their treatment, but few take this further. In Hugh's case the bitterness and rancour was to well up and find focus in two directions: a flagrant disregard for the laws which had made him an outcast, and the impetus to perform every act of treachery against the chief which opportunity presented.

Some four years later the first of these opportunities for Hugh to revenge himself upon the young chief arose. Donald Gorm had just attained his majority and was sailing with his followers to visit Angus of Dunnyveg when unfavourable winds drove him into Loch Tarbet, Jura. The loch marked the division between the lands of MacLean and MacDonald of Dunnyveg, and Donald was lying on the MacLean side. Hugh, who was still outlawed, had embarked on a career of piracy and, being anchored nearby, craftily saw a means of causing trouble for the MacDonalds. Landing a party of his men to round up some MacLean cattle, they were lifted aboard and the sails set leaving suspicion to fall upon the MacDonalds. The scheme worked and the MacLeans set upon the smaller band and killed a great many. Donald survived only because he had chosen to sleep on board his birlinn. The ensuing feud was to extend over the following thirteen years, marked by numerous bloody conflicts and a great loss of life. This of course did not unsettle Hugh who, continuing his trade of piracy, was wreaking havoc with the West Coast trade. The Fife fishermen were but one group to pour out their complaints to the Privy Council, whose summons for Hugh to appear before them naturally went unheeded.

That he should have been granted in 1589 a remission for his crimes against the MacLeans is remarkable enough; that he should appear in the same year as the steward of Trotternish is astounding. Apparently his lawless nature and violent conduct resulted in a very short tenure but a long-remembered experience for those who had been touched by his stewardship.

That Hugh figured high on the list of men wanted by the Government is plain from their specific requirement that Hugh, 'and no other' was to be held as hostage for retaining Caisteal Camus as a royal castle. There is no record of him ever being held though, and, now advanced in years, he was soon reverting to his piratical ways. In

1600, Thomas Inglis, a merchant burgess of Edinburgh, complained that Hugh had boarded one of his ships in Loch Shiel, Lewis, and 'wranguslie, violentlie and maisterful against all order of law or justice, reft, spuilzeit, intromettit with, and away tuke fra thaim the forsaid schip with the whole merchandise, goods, and gear'.

In 1601 the MacLeods of Dunvegan and the MacDonalds of Sleat made their peace. Possibly as a result of this Hugh felt able to return to Skye. That he seems to have come to some understanding with his chief is clear from the fact that he was permitted to build his rectangular tower at Cuidreach. However, it was perhaps too much to expect a nature steeped in over five decades of misdeeds capable of such immediate reformation. As the castle was nearing completion Hugh was busy plotting a bloody overthrow of the chief and leading members of the clan, which would bring the chiefship into his own hands. The magnitude of the plan was too great for even one so evil to accomplish alone, and, covertly, he set sail for Uist in his birlinn to enlist the aid of all who might share his hatred of the chief. The massacre was planned to take place at the house-warming celebrating the completion of Caisteal Uisdean, and party to the plot was one William Martin, tenant in Trotternish. Tradition relates that the scheme was only uncovered in time through a careless slip by Hugh when sending out the invitations to the feast. Apparently a letter to his chief expressing his loyalty and allegiance and one to William Martin, his accomplice, were misdirected. When Donald Gorm read of what his kinsman intended he commissioned Donald of Eriskay to bring him to Duntulm dead or alive. Hotly pursued Hugh took refuge at the fort of Dun na Sticir, situated on an island in a lake in North Uist, and accessible only by a secret ford. Besieged by Donald for several weeks, Hugh and his men apparently suffered terrible privations. It seems that they were dependant for food upon an old woman who, on the darkest of nights, arrived by the secret route with a sack of unground corn. One night she stayed longer than usual, and was observed by the besiegers being conducted by Hugh across the stepping stones to the shore. With the path now revealed, the way was open for Donald's men to take the fort. All Hugh's men were taken and bound, but of Hugh himself there was no sign. An old woman discovered grinding the corn was questioned at length and eventually unmasked as Hugh attired in women's clothes. The deception was apparently discovered when Donald threw the 'old crone' a piece of bread, and instead of spreading the knees to catch it in the skirt as a woman might,

Hugh brought his knees together to trap it as a man would naturally do.

On being brought before his chief, Donald Gorm Mor ironically commended him for the house-warming that had been planned, and that it was now the turn of Hugh to be the Chief's guest – for the remainder of his days. Cast into the dungeon of Duntulm, Hugh could make out in the grey light of his cell a platter of beef and a jug. With an appetite sharpened by his recent privations he made short work of the beef, though it was strangely salty. Taking the jug with which to slake his thirst, to his horror he discovered that it was empty. His sufferings and the agonies of despair to which he was driven were only revealed years afterwards when the vault was opened. Within lay the skeleton of a man holding in his bony hand a pewter jug crunched and broken by jaws in a final maddening frenzy of thirst. Two centuries later the Reverend Alexander MacGregor of Kilmuir noted that the skull and thighbones of Hugh lay for many years in a window of the parish church. Owing to their extraordinary size they were great objects of curiosity until eventually they were interred in 1827, finally laying to rest Hugh MacMallach Chloinn Uisdean ('the arch-demon of Clan Donald').


DESCRIPTION

*Caisteal Uisdean* was the last of the true mediaeval 'castles' to be raised on the island. In the spirit of its namesake it stands as a gaunt cheerless rectangle, precariously perched within a metre of a sheer cliff-drop to the sea below, and devoid of any redeeming architectural embellishment.

The building is a rectangle, measuring 15m. by 10m. It is orientated with its long-axis so nearly due east–west, that it will be regarded as such for ease of description. The walls are constructed of locally quarried massive basalt blocks, pinned with smaller pieces and bonded with a heavy lime mortar. Varying between 2–2.6m. in thickness they survive in places to a height of 4.3m. The severity of its construction might alone discourage the less determined from assailing it; certainly the doorway set 3m. from the ground in the centre of the west wall offers the visitor little hope of access by this means. A more prudent, if nevertheless still energetic, means of entry is to be found via the window at basement level in the north wall.

The interior of *Caisteal Uisdean* from the south-east angle. The entrance, with its stair to the floor above, lies in the far wall.

## THE BASEMENT

Although the interior is strewn with rubble, the height of the window ledges suggest that the original floor level lies not far below the surface. A timber ceiling covered this large rectangular room, the joists being seated on narrow ledges along the north and south walls. A space 10.3m. by 5.4m. was lit by only two loops, or windows. One of these (that giving access today) lies near the western end of the north wall, with the other near the eastern end of the south wall. Both are of similar construction, with a wide splay entering just above floor level leading beneath arched vaulting to a breast at the mid-thickness of the wall. From here to the outer face the inward splay of the loop is capped by a rough segmental arch. The light in the north wall differs only in respect of a single step before the breast. Just above this window and adjacent to the west is a small opening that continues through the thickness of the wall to the outer face. Its purpose is unclear.

Access between this basement and the floor above is likely to have been by means of a wooden stair. From the position of the openings at first-floor level this would have been most conveniently placed within the south-west corner.

## THE FIRST-FLOOR LEVEL

Access to the door set high in the west wall was probably by means of wooden steps which, in the event of an assault, could be drawn up or even cast over the cliff edge. A stone-edged channel runs from the cliff-edge directly below the doorway and appears to have been the seating for such a construction. The doorway is 1.15m. in width, leading within the wall to where a stout wooden door once closed from the north against deep checks. Open, it rested against the slight inward splay of the north wall of the entrance passage. The entrance passage opens into a spacious hall of similar dimensions to that below. Here, the provision for lighting is more generous, with windows in all except the west wall.

The north and east wall are each pierced by a single window, that in the north wall lying near its western end and directly above the basement loop. The eastern window lies directly opposite the door and would have admitted the first light of the morning into the hall. The south wall may have been lit by two windows, one near its eastern end, with possibly a second near the western end. The first-floor windows are broadly similar, differing from those below in not having splayed interiors. Each appears to have the remnants of either a single step or the lowest course of a breast within the embrasure, but all are now so damaged that their form thereafter is conjectural.

A fireplace over a metre in width lies towards the eastern end of the north wall. Part of the corbelling at the shoulder, and where it narrows to join the flue, survives; the hearth is set above the ledge carrying floor joists and these were presumably protected from stray embers by some means such as flagging.

## THE SECOND FLOOR

Midway along the south wall of the entrance passage, a narrow flight of stairs leads upwards within the thickness of the wall. This ascent, by the steep and narrow corridor, is all that remains of the third chamber above first-floor level. While its dimensions presumably mirrored those below, its arrangements and the form of the roof it once carried are now lost.

One rather unreliable source claims that the building was never completed, yet, as the occasion for Hugh's incarceration pivots on the house-warming feast, Hugh certainly cannot be considered as ever having taken up formal residence here. From the silence of the sources thereafter the building seems to have remained unoccupied.

OCHEL CASTLE, seen from the east, as it
y have appeared in the later 16th century.
e reconstruction is based on the surviving
n, the views of William Daniell and the
blished photographic record made by the
CAHMS, disregarding the engraving after Sir
omas Dick Lauder.

The entrance has been reconstructed to
e the small chamber over it described by
swell. On the right, the outcrop has been
wn cased in stonework to support the upper
rtyard and curtain; there is some evidence
this in the cutting back of the rockface.

There are several possible routes for the external
steps down the rock from the entrance, those
shown follow the practice of putting the
entrance route below the strongest defence, here
in the north-west tower. The positions of the
chimneys on the north-east and south-east
towers are conjectural.

The problem of access from the lower
courtyard to the upper could only have been
solved by two solutions; a stair from the kitchen,
or one from the south-east tower and gate-
house chamber. A wooden stair from the
kitchen is quite out of the question despite signs

of a stair leading down from the upper
courtyard into the chamber over the kitchen.
Imagination might suggest that this continued
down into the cramped kitchen but this is
clearly impossible because of lack of room and
the disposition of built-in features. A short stair
through Boswell's chamber, from the upper floor
of the south-east tower, is used here as the only
solution giving access from the lower courtyard
to the upper, an expression of Bastard Feudalism
perhaps. (Watercolour, by David Roberts)

CAISTEAL CAMUS shown as it may have appeared during its latest phase in the 1630s. By this time the new house had been built along the lines seen in other castles in the district. The mural windows are all known to have existed but the dormers are entirely conjectural. The gable-end stack is suggested by still exist. A garden has been shown divided by paths following the lines of earlier building shown in the ground plan.

The long rectangular tower has conjectural dormer windows. The machicolation and bartizans are interpreted from McCulloch and those seen on most of the nearby castles. It that at Dunvegan, but it has here been shown undergoing repair to its roof. In the background is activity suggesting the pastoral nature of Skye's economy; the run-rig shown in the background is still clearly visible.

(Watercolour, by David Roberts)

View of CAISTEAL MAOL as it might have appeared in 1600. The level above the first floor is conjectural. (Watercolour, by David Roberts)

CAISTEAL UISDEAN shown during the bitter winter of 1620 when in parts of Scotland sheep-flocks were reduced from thousands to handfuls. Its appearance is much as floor has been supplied by the artist and a corbelled-out merlon has been added as the likely addition to the defence of the first-floor entrance and conjectural wooden steps.

A view of DUN SGATHAICH as it may have appeared in the 1570s.

The view is from the east. On the upper level is the curtain wall flanked by the gate-house tower to the south and another tower to the north. Just showing to the south of the gate-house is the curtain running westwards to a small garderobe turret. A corbelled turret is shown projecting slightly in front of the wall over the main gate through the curtain. There is no evidence for this but such a device was often

employed so that missiles could be dropped on the heads of the besieger. Leading down from these main defences is the walled forestair to the draw-bridge over the steep-sided dry moat. The design of the walls of the stair is simple but sophisticated. They still survive in places to a height of some 3m. sufficient to show that they followed a stepped profile between slight masonry piers never intended to carry a roof or defensive platform. Between the piers the wall was feathered to the top edge and, no doubt, the piers were conically capped to deny a foothold

to an attacker attempting to use them as 'stepping stones' to the upper level. The design placed the sloping faces on the outside where they would catch the light in an attractive way rather than placing them on the inside where they would have been a surprise deterrent. Only three loops survive,one to the north of the drawbridge capstan-house and two in the east face of the upper section; it was, therefore, only a hindrance to the attacker rather than a front-line defence of the 'strengthie castell'.
(Watercolour, by David Roberts)

David T. Richardson

DUNTULM CASTLE is shown in early April 1635 with cottars and boonmen preparing ground for crops. The castle had by then been remodelled with a new curtain and bastions for artillery, the new wing had been added to the dowed. Early topographical views allow an accurate reconstruction of the now-jumbled ruin. The ground plan, from bastions to curtain and tower footings, is still there for us to enjoy in the most dramatic of settings.

DUNVEGAN CASTLE is seen here from the west as it may have been early in 1684. A mason's lean-to lodge has already been built preparatory to the building of *Iain Breac's* new wing. The stone figure (now preserved in the castle) intended to support a sundial is shown in a conjectural position amidst equally imaginary knot-

gardens in the Gun Court. It has been assumed that wooden mullioned and transomed windows had been installed throughout by this time. The Fairy Tower now formed part of the hall range built in 1623 but the tower and jamb were still separated from them by a narrow alley. The scale and position of the hall-range

frontage is accurate but the detailing is conjectural, being drawn from contemporary models. The wall of the Gun Court reflects the surviving masonry but it may well be that a gate-house and ancillary structures like those of Duntulm await archaelogical investigation. (Watercolour, by David Roberts)

EILEAN DONAN Castle is seen as it was before 1654. Accurate reconstruction has been made easier by the wealth of survey and pictorial information. The heptagonal bastion was intended as an artillery platform by which a field of fire could cover the old entrance now shielded by outworks. (Watercolour, by David Roberts)

# Clachan

NG 5463 3660

PORTREE PARISH

There are a number of early references which indicate that a three-storey tower house stood in what is now the garden at the rear of Raasay House. It is first recorded by Dean Monro in 1549 as '. . . the castell of Kilmaluok [Kilmaluag] . . . with a fair orcheartis . . .' In 1705 Martin Martin noted that MacLeod had his seat at Clachan which was 'adorned with a little tower'.

Until the 17th century the main residence of the MacLeods of Raasay lay at Brochel Castle, and the tower house at Clachan probably functioned originally only as a subsidiary residence in much the same manner as Caisteal Camus did for the MacDonalds in Sleat. After the death of Iain Garbh the Chief, whose tragic death by drowning, 'after a rant of drinking uppon the shoare' was widely lamented, Brochel was abandoned as the family seat in preference for Clachan. Presumably the tower house now became the chief residence, although by 1745 the accommodation was evidently unsatisfactory, and a new house was built. Shortly after, the tower was demolished.

Whether the tower building really justified Dean Monro's description as a castle is uncertain, for no illustrations or more detailed descriptions exist. Perhaps a more reliable indication of its value as a military stronghold lies in the survey of revenue and fighting power undertaken between 1577 and 1595 in connection with James VI's Highland policy: here no mention is made of the tower whatsoever.

Raasay House from the east looking across the Sound of Raasay to Ben Lee in 1813. The tower at *Clachan* formerly stood to the rear of the house, shown in the foreground of this detail from an aquatint by William Daniell.

# Dun Ringill

NG 5619 1708

STRATH PARISH

ROUTE

Dun Ringill from the north-west. The ditch hollow lies to the bottom left. Beyond this the outer stone apron flanking the approach runs back to the outer wall-face of the Iron Age structure. The lintels have been removed from the original passage and built into a new passage extension at the rear beneath a curtain 'breastwork'.

Take the A881 road from Broadford to Elgol as far as Kilmarie. Park here, or at a point down the minor road on the left which will cause no inconvenience to traffic, and certainly well before the entrance leading to Kilmarie House. Walk almost to the house gates, turning left through a gate leading to the bridge across the river. Cross the bridge, turn right, passing a large stone cairn built over 5,000 years ago later used for Bronze Age burials around 2200–1800 BC. Follow the footpath around the coast to the fort at Dun Ringill.

## HISTORY

It may seem strange to be including in a book on castles a structure which so evidently proclaims its Iron Age origins. Its narrow entrance passage with door-checks and bar-holes, intra-mural cell and drystone construction are all characteristics familiarly associated with brochs built some 2,000 years ago. This site is singled out from the many other prehistoric sites of similar form and construction by considerable evidence of refurbishment at a later date. This was clearly intended to revive its defensive role, and presumably served to protect the pair of buildings constructed within. This re-occupation might have taken place at any time following the abandonment of the site by the original builders. On the basis of the remains alone it would indeed be difficult to determine with conviction which of the traditional building periods – early Christian, Scandinavian, or later mediaeval – to which this rebuilding work may be assigned. Tradition, however, relates that Dun Ringill was occupied by the Clan MacKinnon long before they held 'Dunakin' or Caisteal Maol as it is known today. Though the story remains unconfirmed by historical texts, the tradition nevertheless is both consistent with other aspects of the clan history, and, moreover, goes some way towards resolving crucial difficulties concerning the territories of the clan and their principal residence.

Through the clan's founder, one Fingon, the MacKinnons could claim descent from Kenneth MacAlpin, the 9th century King of Dalriada, whose annexation of the Pictish territories laid the foundations of the mediaeval Scottish kingdom. By the mid-14th century the clan held extensive territories on both Mull and Skye. However, it was from their possession of Strathairdle on Skye by which the chiefs were known. As late as 1542 their main dwelling was said to lie within an area extending from Strathaird on the west along the 'Strath' or plain to Broadford in the east. In an Act of Council of 1360 their main dwelling is called Castle Findanus, from a Latinizing of the eponymous founder, Fingon. It is not made clear which of the two castles known to have belonged to the MacKinnons was the 'Castle Findanus' of the Act. It might be argued that it is unlikely to have been Caisteal Maol as the remains there appear to date from no earlier than the 15th century; besides which, towards the end of its life at least, it was known not as Castle Findanus but Dunakin. Even the most cursory acquaintance with the complex currents underlying the history of castles in

A view of the Iron Age passageway looking east towards the internal thickening of the defensive wall. This contains the new passage reutilising the lintels of its predecessor. An attacker would have been vulnerable to fire from above and would also have met a stout wooden door at the beginning of the covered passage. At the rear, steps rise up to the level within.

Skye and Lochalsh make seemingly logical conclusions meaningless. As with so many of the castles elsewhere on Skye, the 15th century work may well mask a predecessor. Equally, Dunakin might be but one of the many names by which it was known; witness, for example, the fort at Duntulm, formerly known as Dun Dhaibhidh, while Caisteal Camus was known variously as Dun Thorovaig, Caisteal Camus, Dun Iaian a Choinnich, Caisteal Ruadh, Caisteal Uaine, and most recently, Knock Castle. Whilst many of these names are clearly the colloquialisms of later generations, it demonstrates the weakness in accepting a name at face value. The main argument against equating Castle Findanus with Caisteal Maol (Dunakin) is that it lies outside the traditional heartland of the clan. The founder's name might be thought more suitably applied to a castle within the home territory, particularly the one claimed by tradition as the chief residence of the MacKinnons, Dun Ringill.

Speculation apart, all that is certain is that Dean Monro records the existence of castles at both Dun Ringill and 'Dunkin' in 1549, and, while it is unclear from his account whether they were then occupied, only the latter is again mentioned in an official report prepared from

Dun Ringill sits on the cliff-edge overlooking the sea. To the north-west are settlement remains comprising field-banks, run-rig and houses. Of the houses lying outside the castle, those shown as a boulder outline may be contemporary with its occupation (M. Wildgoose, and based upon RCAHMS).

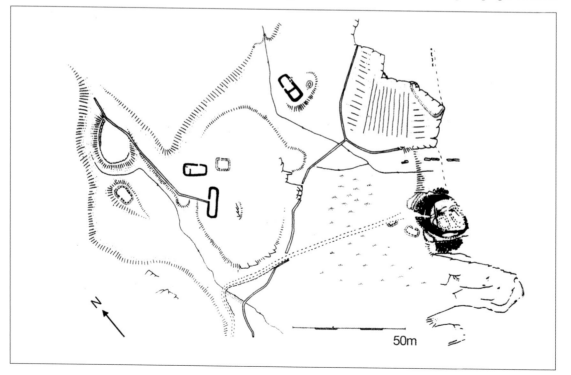

50m

James VI sometime between 1577 and 1595. By the later 16th century at least, the MacKinnons had abandoned their traditional family seat for the more imposing and commodious residence overlooking the Kyle.

## DESCRIPTION

Dun Ringill occupies the stumpy promontory of Jurassic sandstone overlooking the beach 14m. below. It is bounded to north and south by steep defiles leading down to the boulder-strewn shoreline and, to the west, by an uneven and frequently boggy terrace containing a complex of houses with associated enclosures. This settlement runs up to the walls of Dun Ringill and while the form and construction of many of these suggest an 18th or 19th century date, other forms may well prove on excavation to have been earlier and, perhaps, contemporary with the mediaeval phase of Dun Ringill.

## THE DITCH

Across the neck of the promontory are traces of a ditch following the curve of the outer wall of the dun. Although the central sector is infilled and now levelled, the ditch cutting is plainly visible at its northern and southern extremities where it runs into the edges of the promontory. Material excavated during its construction and subsequent cleaning out has left a small linear bank along its western edge. To the south-west of the entrance the ditch infill is overlaid by a later rectangular building erected, no doubt, long after Dun Ringill had been abandoned.

## THE IRON AGE CORE

At the heart of this construction lies the remains of the Iron Age dun, a defensive fortification built some 2,000 years ago. Whilst lacking the circular form of the true broch, Dun Ringill contains many features found in brochs, such as the rising mural passages, chambers set within the thickness of the wall, and the long narrow entrance to the interior with checks for a wooden door having bar-holes behind. The defences appear to have been left uncompleted on the seaward side for, at its north-eastern extremity, the wall seems to terminate in an abrupt butt-end. Perhaps the steep and high cliff-face on this side was considered to have been a sufficiently daunting obstacle to attack. On the landward side the wall thickness increases to 4.6m. where it is pierced by a long narrow passage giving access to the interior. Just within the entrance lie the wall-checks, L-shaped constructions against which the door would close, protecting the door edges from being prised away from the wall with levers. A stout wooden bar held the gate secure. The bar-holes for this beam lie just within the passage beyond the door-checks. This passage was formerly roofed with large lintels but, in the mediaeval period, the wall was lowered and the lintels removed. These were used in the passage added at the rear of the former dun passage.

On the interior wall above and to either side of the original entrance to the interior are the remains of two vertical openings extending through the inner wall-leaf to a mural passage sited well above Iron Age ground level, these may correspond to the vertical openings in brochs elsewhere, and are generally regarded as a device used to relieve the weight of superincumbent masonry.

From the interior an opening in the south wall led to a narrow passage leading westwards to a long and high corbelled cell. The outer wall of this cell has now fallen away although it may well have been intact during the mediaeval occupation.

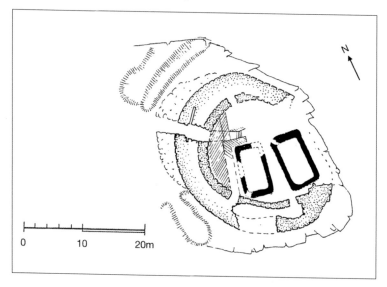

Plan of Dun Ringill.

## MEDIAEVAL REOCCUPATION

In the early Middle Ages this Iron Age structure was refortified and became traditionally the residence of the clan chief of the MacKinnons. A low wall was built from the inner face of the ditch to the southern corner of the entrance. The Iron Age passage walls were reduced to a height of some 1.5m. This cutting was revetted left and right by walls set back from the old face. This created a deep and narrow approach to a new doorway and passage set to the rear of the Iron Age entrance.

Inside the dun only as much occupation debris was removed necessary to support a chord-wall infill against the passage entrance. This semi-circular abutment was built of lime-mortared rubble stone. The abutment was pierced by a continuation of the old passage line, but had its own door-check. A steep flight of steps leads up from the inner opening of the passage to give access to a new level established on the old debris. Revetments left and right of the steps prevented debris from falling into the cutting. Across the top of this chord-wall is evidence for a low narrow wall and a ledge 0.8m. in width towards the interior. This may have formed a parapet walk and breastwork in defending the entrance, a crude, but no doubt effective, device of the sort given more competent architectural expression elsewhere on Skye.

## INTERNAL BUILDINGS

The southern part of the interior is wholly taken up with two sub-rectangular buildings. Orientated lengthways north to south, they have rounded corners inside and out. A narrow passage between them leads to the doorway of the cell in the south wall. Both buildings measure 4.5m. x 2.4m. internally with gable walls 1m. in thickness with the side-walls being slightly thinner. Presumably doorways were set in the gable ends. There is little reason for doubting these buildings to have been contemporary with mediaeval occupation at Dun Ringill.

# Dun Sgathaich

NG 5952 1207

SLEAT PARISH

## ROUTE

Turn off the Broadford–Ardvasar Road (A851) where the signs to Ord
and Tokavaig indicate, parking near the eastern end of Ob Gauscavaig,
the bay lying to the west of Tokavaig. The castle is approached by foot
around the eastern shore of the bay. Access to the castle via the
outworks is, however, treacherous and the remains are in a sufficiently
dangerous condition as to recommend viewing only from the safety of
the mainland rock.

*Dun Sgathaich* looking from the south
across Loch Slapin with the hills of
Strathaird in the background.

## HISTORY

Embedded within the rich oral tradition of Celtic society are threads that extend back to very remote times indeed. The handful of epic traditions which have survived tell of an heroic society led by a class of warriors; of their adventures, battles and frailties in a world decidedly *pre*-historic and long before the advent of Christianity. Passed down orally by a professional class of *seannachies* or story-tellers, they were later recorded by mediaeval writers and presented as though the people did once exist and that the events which befell them actually took place. While to the modern ear the realism is difficult to sustain in the face of fantastic exaggeration, or when events of a patently supernatural kind occur, nevertheless the strength of belief in such stories by earlier generations is confirmed in the countless landscape features associated by name with these ancient heroes. Here, both on Skye and the mainland, may be found numerous references to Diarmad, friend of the great Irish hero Finn and his warrior band (Dun Diarmad, near Struan; Diarmad's Grave at Braes, Glendale and Kintail). Finn himself was said to have rested when hunting at Suidh Finn (Finn's seat), near Portree, and to have had his hearth at the prehistoric standing stones at Kensaleyre called Sornaichean Chor Fhinn (Finn's hearth). Best known of all the great heroes associated with Skye was Cú Chulainn, the legendary Ulster warrior who journeyed to Skye to complete his training in arms. His destination was Dun Sgathaich (Fort of Shadow) where the warrior-queen, Sgathaich, trained men in the art of fighting. Cú Chulainn's journey was long and fraught with dangers but each was overcome in turn. At last he reached the castle, separated from the main body of rock by a yawning chasm and linked only by a perilous bridge that threw off all who failed to get across in two strides. Twice Cú Chulainn tried to cross without success, but the third time he succeeded. After knocking on the door so hard that his spear shaft pierced the timbers, he was finally admitted by Uathach (Spectre), the daughter of Sgathaich. His training was long and difficult and while staying at Dun Sgathaich many adventures befell him. Most versions recount how conflict arose between Sgathaich and a neighbouring princess, Aife (Reflection). To ensure his safety during the hostilities Sgathaich gave Cú Chulainn a sleeping potion to bind him for 24 hours. However, he awoke after only an hour and appeared on the field of battle to champion the

The causeway and steep stairway leading to the castle gate.

queen against Aife. The combat between the two was fearsome but eventually Cú Chulainn's sword was splintered by a heavy blow and it seemed as if he were lost. Quickly he caused a distraction by shouting that Aife's favourite chariot and horses were in danger. Thus distracted the queen was slung over Cú Chulainn's shoulder and carried off the field. In addition to extracting a promise from Aife that she would never again fight with Queen Sgathaich, Aife bore Cú Chulainn a son, Conlai. In the fullness of time Conlai journeyed to Ireland to see his father, but this is quite another story.

One Skye legend, apparently of much later date, conflicts with the more popular version which has the castle built by Cú Chulainn in a single night! This relates how:

> All night the witch sang and the castle grew
> Up from the rock, with the tower and turrets crowned;
> All night she sang, when fell the morning dew
> 'Twas finished round and round.

The castle at Dun Sgathaich does not emerge again in island history until the 14th century, at which time Sleat formed part of the patrimony of the Earl of Ross and was held by the MacLeods of Dunvegan as vassals of the Earl. The MacAskills reputedly acted as hereditary wardens of the castle, a position held since the days when the Western Isles were governed by the Norse Kings of Man. Yet in the turbulent political undercurrents of the later 14th and 15th centuries, events were to see a new family established in the district, irreversibly changing the older order. It is clear that the MacDonalds, as Lords of the Isles, long coveted gaining a foothold in Skye. Donald of Harlaw, 2nd Lord of the Isles, invaded Skye in 1395, but his forces were severely beaten by a large body of MacLeods who afterwards collected and numbered the heads of the slain, and had them despatched to Dunvegan Castle as trophies. It seems, however, that the MacDonalds might not have been so completely repulsed as the MacLeods historian suggests, for it is possible that Donald's half-brother Godfrey occupied Sleat for a while and was resident in Dun Sgathaich from 1389 until 1401.

The premature death of William, 4th Chief of the MacLeods, offered the MacDonalds yet further opportunity to establish a foothold in Sleat. William's son was a minor and under the mismanagement of the regent appointed, Ian the Truculent, the MacLeods splintered into factions weakening their defences against hostile outside forces. Seizing the moment, the MacDonalds again raided Sleat, seizing both Caisteal Camus and Dun Sgathaich. Yet once more the MacLeods drew together and successfully repulsed the invaders.

During the early decades of the 15th century the castle was seized by James I. This was in response to an insurrection against the Crown, headed by Donald Balloch, cousin of the Lord of the Isles, who at that time was being held prisoner of the King at Tantallon Castle in East Lothian. Both Dun Sgathaich and Caisteal Camus were seized by James in 1431, although matters soon returned to normal – for a few decades more at least!

In 1469 the situation altered radically, when Hugh, brother of John, 10th Lord of the Isles, received a grant of 28 merklands in Sleat. Thereafter he was known as 'Hugh of Sleat' and it was through him that the MacDonalds of Sleat claimed descent. His possession was confirmed by royal charter in 1495 and, though Dun Sgathaich is not mentioned, it may reasonably be assumed that this castle had become the chief residence of the Sleat MacDonalds. Hugh died in 1498 and was succeeded by his eldest son John. Having no heirs of his own and apparently determined that the estate should not fall into the hands of his half-brothers, John set about a reckless attempt to alienate the patrimony. Amongst the properties he disposed of were some 20 merklands in Sleat together with the 'castro et fortalicio de Dunskahay', here first mentioned by name in a charter of confirmation, dated 1505, to 'Ranaldo Alansoun de Ylandturim'.

In 1505 John died and his half brother, Donald Gallach, succeeded to the sadly reduced patrimony. Despite the grants to Ranald Alansoun and others, Donald occupied Dun Sgathaich and continued to claim possession of the lands alienated by his predecessor. However, he was soon embroiled in a vicious cycle of fratricide, fostered largely by Gillespic Dubh, a half-brother who felt that he was being overlooked by the chief. Gillespic first arranged the death of one half-brother, Donald Herrach, by an ingenious trick: a competition to see who could leap highest and touch a rope-noose with his nose. When Donald leapt the noose was dropped around his neck and hot irons were thrust through his bowels. Gillespic hastened to Dun Sgathaich before news of the deed reached his chief. He was made welcome and taken to inspect a galley which the chief was building. Drawing Donald's attention to an imaginary defect, Gillespic took the opportunity to stab him. Mortally wounded, Donald implored Gillespic to spare his son and it seems that the murderer was indeed so stricken with remorse at his evil actions that he took his nephews under his protection. On 6th April 1508 Gillespic received a crown pardon for 'ye slauchter of Umquhile Donald Hutchonsoun (Uisdean) of the Ilis'.

Just five years later the chief's residence became once again a pawn in the protracted struggle between the island chiefs and the Crown. The death of James IV at Flodden Field in September 1513 appeared to present an opportunity to re-establish the Lordship of the Isles surrendered to the King in 1494. At a gathering at Caisteal Maol many of the chiefs had given their support to Sir Donald MacDonald of Lochalsh. Donald Gruamach, the future chief of the MacDonalds of Sleat, was still a minor at the time this rising took place, staying in the house of the Earl of Moray. It is not known who was then resident at Dun Sgathaich, although it may have been his uncle, Gillespic Dubh. One source suggests that the castle was at the time forfeited to the Crown, a situation which would explain why it was besieged by the rebellious chiefs led by the MacLeods of Dunvegan and Harris. Support for Sir Donald was short-lived as the Regency flexed its

The two arched walls that straddle the 'yawning chasm' and carry the drawbridge.

considerable political and military muscle and, by 1515, those involved in 'the tresonable segeing and taking of the kingis castillis and house of Carnebog [Treshnish Isles] and Dunskaith' were pardoned.

By 1518 Donald Gruamach assumed the leadership of the clan, having first avenged the death of his father by stabbing his uncle, Gillespic Dubh, while he slept. A bond of manrent signed in 1521 by 'Donald of Dunscagth' shows him resident in the castle with his first wife, Catherine. He was visited here by his cousin and close friend

Ranald Herrach. Both men were closely bonded through the loss of their fathers at the hands of Gillespic Dubh and, while Ranald was pleased to see his cousin, he was far from taken with the relatives of the chief's wife. It seemed to Ranald that their haughty manner and utter lack of deference to their host required immediate action. Under the cloak of night Ranald crept by each bed in turn, despatching its occupant until twelve of the chief's wife's kinfolk lay dead. The bodies were thrown out the window onto the rocks below. At first light Ranald prepared to leave the castle. His chief urged him to stay, or at least delay, until his wife came down. To this Ranald replied that he must leave instantly 'for she will not bless me when she looks out her window and views my morning's work'. Such was the case, for shortly after an assassin hired by the chief's wife to avenge the deaths caught up with Ranald at Griminish in Uist and murdered him.

Donald Gruamach was still in residence at Dun Sgathaich in 1531 when ordered to appear before the King at Edinburgh. He was later succeeded in 1534 by his son Donald Gorm. It has been said that, following the death of the latter in 1539, the chief's residence was moved to Duntulm in Trotternish. Such a claim however finds little support in the historical record. In 1549 Dean Monro refers to the 'castill of Dunskay perteining to the said Donald Gromsone'

Plan of Dun Sgathaich (based upon RCAHMS).

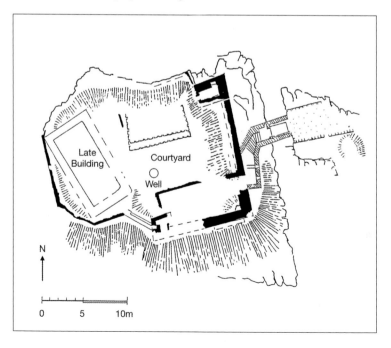

[Gormson]. Twenty-three years later this same chief signed an obligation to the Bishop of the Isles on 16th January 1572 at 'Dounsceiche'. In a description of the Isles compiled between 1577 and 1595 Dun Sgathaich is noted as one of 'twa strengthie castells in Slait', hardly a description of an abandoned and derelict stronghold. Indeed it was only in 1618, when the long-coveted possession of Trotternish depended upon Duntulm as the MacDonalds' main residence, that the impetus to move became justified. The castle which had reputedly witnessed the training of one of the West's most powerful folk heroes, and had been in continuous occupation for over five centuries to a succession of MacAskills, MacLeods and MacDonalds, was finally shed like a cocoon by a world which had now moved over the threshold of a new order.

## DESCRIPTION

The rock on which the castle stands is approached from the east by a broad revetted platform leading to a deep cleft 5m. in width separating it from the parent mass. The two arched walls flung across this cutting formerly carried a wooden drawbridge, the pivot-holes for which are plainly visible on the castle side. Behind the drawbridge are the checks for a stout door which, when opened, gave access to a rising flight of steps. These are flanked by walls pierced with narrow loops on the eastern side. This whole approach to the castle gate is of late construction, the drawbridge elements perhaps replacing an earlier form.

The castle complex is now ruinous and appears to have been partially cleared away at some time following abandonment. Many features remain either hidden or only faintly visible. While rebuilding and additions have undoubtedly taken place here, the scale of the works and their sequence will only be revealed through excavation.

At the stairhead lies the entrance passage through the curtain wall. Above this would have been a continuation of the parapet walk, possibly carried by a gate-house structure to protect the point of greatest weakness in the castle defences. At the south-east angle are the remains of a stair within the tower which perhaps gave access to this curtain-wall walkway.

The whole summit of the rock measures only 23m. x 17m. and

the stout curtain wall of the castle follows very closely the irregular edge of the plateau. To the west the curtain wall is neither as regular nor as complete as that to the east. The latter seems to mark a separate and later construction, giving added strength to the landward frontage. At either end of this reversed L-shaped refurbishment are small towers, each containing a garderobe, or privy, at ground-floor level. The character of the stonework of this refurbishment is reminiscent of that in the 16th-century phase 3 at Eilean Donan. In part it is built up from earlier courses of masonry at its base.

The curtain wall encloses an area of only some 300 square metres. Most of this appears to have been taken up with buildings on all sides except perhaps that to the east. The open courtyard contains a small well. South of the well is a revetment or a wall-footing aligned west-east. This encloses what appears to have been a narrow sunken entrance court against the south curtain. To the north of the well is a raised square platform, its southern wall-face stepped back from a low footing. It might be suggested that this site was formerly occupied by a tower. The absence of such a tower would make Dun Sgathaich unique amongst the castles of the district.

A single-storey rectangular building lay to the west of the courtyard. Its ruin measures 11m. x 6m. with walls only a metre in width. A doorway lies near the southern end of the eastern wall. Relative to the other structural elements it remains in a condition which suggests that it was built late in the castle's history. Its proportions indicate that it might be a crude imitation of the later 16th- or early 17th-century halls raised within castle enclosures, perhaps overlying the site of earlier buildings.

# Duntulm Castle

NG 4098 7434

KILMUIR PARISH

ROUTE

Follow the A856 road northwards along the western side of Trotternish, turning off at Uig to follow the A855. At the hairpin at Duntulm, park in the car park on the western side of the road. Continue on foot through the gateway indicated, along the footpath to the castle.

HISTORY

The castle of Duntulm stands on a desolate basalt promontory 30m above the pounding seas below. Navigating its broken defences and crumbling walls, a vivid imagination is required to reconstruct the

*Below.* Detail from a later 19th-century photograph of the castle from the south by the studio of George Washington Wilson. It shows just how much of the castle has been lost in the brief space of a century. On the right, the tall remnant of the tower, illustrated by MacGibbon & Ross, has gone and, in the gales of January 1990 the northern tower (the central upstand in the photograph) was also lost.

*Left.* View of the castle from the south, taken in 1985.

former splendour of the home of the MacDonald Chiefs. It is said that the mediaeval castle was built on the ruins of a much earlier fort, possibly one of the many Iron Age duns sited on rocky headlands and promontories around the coastline. This same tradition also records that in former times the fort was known as 'Dun Dhaibhidh', David's Fort, after a Norse chief who resided here when the western seaboard was ruled by the Kings of Norway. David the White appears in Njal's Saga as being active in Fair Isle at the beginning of the 11th century, and perhaps it was he, or some namesake, who occupied the promontory.

Norse control was formally ended by the Treaty of Perth in 1266 and thereafter the castle and lands of Trotternish frequently changed hands, sometimes held by the Lordship of the Isles and sometimes by the Earls of Ross. For much of the time it was held by the MacLeods as vassals of the Earls of Ross. By this time the castle was known as Duntulm, probably a toponymic reference to the island (or 'holm' in Scandinavian) which lay adjacent. Hardening the soft consonant H to T is characteristic of the Gaelic tongue, and, while a similar word, *Tòlm* occurs in Gaelic with the meaning of 'a grassy hillock', the more unusual feature is perhaps more likely to find a place in the name than the commonplace.

By the year 1476 John, Lord of the Isles, had effectively surrendered his powers to the King. John's son and heir, Angus Og, was fiercely resentful of his loss of birthright and embarked on an heroic but futile attempt to recover his heritage. By 1482 Angus had raided Trotternish and seized Duntulm, for he now styled himself 'Lord of Trotternish'. Three years later his name appears again on a charter to the monks of Iona as 'Master of the Isles and Lord of Trotternish'. When Angus died in 1490 his lands and possessions were claimed by his uncle, Hugh of Sleat. Hugh's claim was a weak one, and while James IV was prepared in 1495 to confirm by charter Hugh's title to the lands of Sleat and the Uists, he was not prepared to alienate those territories he believed to have passed to the Crown with the surrender of the Lordship of the Isles. With the MacDonald claim tacitly rejected it was the turn of the MacLeods to make a bid for lands traditionally held by them. In 1498 Alasdair Crotach sought to secure his claim to Trotternish, but received merely its stewardship and confirmation of a holding of two unciates of land in the district.

Just four months later, the remainder of Trotternish, together with

Duntulm, was granted to Torquhil MacLeod of Lewis.

Throughout the course of the 16th century Trotternish appears, as we shall see, to have been used as an important pawn in the Crown's attempt to maintain a balanced control with the MacLeod and MacDonald chiefdoms. In 1509 the baliary of Trotternish was taken away from Alasdair Crotach MacLeod and granted to Gillespic Dubh, the son of Hugh of Sleat through a union with the daughter of Torquhil MacLeod of Lewis. It seems that Alasdair Crotach later regained the stewardship only to be forcibly ejected from both the office and the lands pertaining to him by Donald Gruamach, 5th Chief of Sleat. This must have occured prior to 1528, for in an attempt to quell a particularly vicious episode of feuding between the MacDonalds and MacLeods, Donald Gruamach was ordered to compensate Alasdair Crotach for unlawfully dispossessing him of the stewardship of Trotternish and the two unciates of land held there by the MacLeods. With commendable persistence the MacLeods returned, only to be ousted again a decade later. Donald Gorm, the 6th Chief of Sleat gathered together a formidable host and launched an attack on both the MacLeods and MacKenzies of Kintail.

By 1541 many of those involved were granted a pardon for their part in the raiding, however, these events had brought home to the Crown the need for effective measures to suppress the mounting disaffection in the Western Highlands. In 1540 a fleet was prepared, and, with the King aboard, the sails were set for the West Coast. It is from this great royal venture that the first specific mention of the castle at Duntulm arises. James V visited Duntulm and was apparently impressed by its commodiousness and strength. Within the decade, Dean Munro

In 1772, Duntulm was visited by Thomas Pennant and his artist Moses Griffiths. Finding the spot sufficiently 'picturesque' Griffiths produced a view which appeared in all subsequent editions of Pennant's *A Voyage to the Hebrides*. He shows the tower (to the left) with the jamb roof to the rear. Abutting these is a lower building with machicolated roof and chimney.

William Daniell was a more able artist than Griffiths although some of his views show an almost careless disregard for details. This view was made in 1819 and shows the castle from the south-west. What appears to have been an entrance is shown near the centre of the small building to the right of the picture.

was to remark on the 'castell of Donntwyline perteining to Donald Gromsome', and some considerable refurbishment might be expected to have taken place, converting whatever former provision existed for a stewardship into a stronghold appropriate to the MacDonald chiefdom.

Whatever the extent of the works undertaken, the MacDonald occupation was not destined to be of long duration. In a 'Description of the Isles', dateable to sometime between 1577 and 1595, it is recorded that, 'Thair was ane castell in Trouterness callit Duncolem quhairof the wallis standis yet'. Clearly the site had by this time been abandoned and possibly the buildings stood unroofed. That the same authority speaks of Dun Sgathaich and Caisteal Camus in a manner which suggests that they were complete and inhabited, forces the conclusion that the chief had returned his residence to Sleat. Indeed, Donald Gormson signed a writ at 'Dounscheiche' on 16th January 1572 and it was probably here that the family returned.

On 17th August 1596, Donald Gorm Mor, the 8th Chief of Sleat, received a five year lease of Trotternish from the Crown. For seventeen years the MacDonalds retained possession until, for some inexplicable reason, the king chose on the 11th January 1613 to grant Sir Rory MacLeod charter rights to the MacDonald lands of Trotternish, Sleat and North Uist. By this charter actual possession of the earth and stone at Duntulm would suffice for possession of all the lands mentioned, and without too long delay Sir Rory took possession on 12th June 1614. For the MacDonalds this was of course an intolerable situation, and one calculated to provoke response. Within a month Donald Gorm Og had secured a new Crown Charter, and on 14th August it was his turn to take possession. So the situation may have continued had a way out of the interminable claim and counter-claim which had been going on for over a century not been resolved by diplomacy. In 1618 both MacDonalds and MacLeods resigned into the King's hands the lands which they held charter. A new charter was drawn up which required Sir Donald Gorm Og, the 9th Chief of Sleat, to make a financial settlement with Sir Rory MacLeod as compensation for any MacLeod claims to Trotternish. Once payment had been made in full, the MacLeods were to withdraw and allow possession by the MacDonalds. Moreover, Sir Donald was thereafter bound to 'mak his residence and dwelling at Duntillum, and, yf he has not a sufficient comelie house ansuerable to his estate alreddy their that he sall with all convenient diligence prepair materiallis and cause build ane civile and comelie house, and yf is house be decayit that he sall repair and mend the same'. Within two years extensive repairs and refurbishments were carried out on buildings abandoned some half a century earlier. In a bond to the Privy Council dated 26th August 1616 implementing a

Line illustration of the chesspiece reputedly found in Loch St. Columba. It is made from walrus tusk and dateable to around the mid-13th century.

meeting of the Highland Chiefs for the peace of the Highlands and Islands, Donald Gorm Og now names Duntulm as his principal residence.

The present condition of the buildings provides few clues as to what repairs and structural additions were undertaken during this period of reoccupation. Fortunately however, a late-19th-century line illustration attests the former existence of corbelling on the south wall of the tower, and a 'revived dog-tooth and nail-head pattern' ornamenting the south-west angle turret. While these features generally date to the 17th century, that the basic structure of the tower should be dated so late is most unlikely. Perhaps it is best to regard these as embellishments of the earlier tower structure. The rectangular building within the north-west angle was certainly in use during this late phase of occupation – perhaps to house the six gentlemen retainers allowed by the Privy Council!

Bloody deeds in the tradition of earlier centuries could and did take place. It was at the beginning of the 17th century when Hugh the

Towards the close of the 19th century a magisterial survey of *The Castellated and Domestic Architecture of Scotland* appeared in five weighty volumes. Its authors, D. MacGibbon and T. Ross, included many fine contemporary illustrations of the buildings. This is one of two views of Duntulm prepared especially for the work, and shows the castle from the west.

Clerk, son of Archibald, was sealed up in one of the underground vaults and left there to die an agonizing death. Nevertheless times were changing as Crown authority was introducing new pressures and influence to bear on subjects in its more remote territories. It is surprising to find in 1628, Sir John MacLeod of Dunvegan, Sir Lachlan MacKinnon of Strath, the Earl of Seaforth, and Alexander MacGillichaluim of Raasay meeting with Sir Donald MacDonald of Sleat at Duntulm. That the matter of the meeting should be to devise a means of preventing poaching by the imposition of fines at law is truly remarkable! While the chiefdoms remained essentially feudal in organization throughout the course of the 17th century, clan infighting was, with but few exceptions, either confined to the level of minor incidents or expressed on a larger scale only within the context of conflicts at a national level.

The changes taking place elsewhere were no less keenly felt at Duntulm, as southern influences pervaded Highland culture. The poetess Mary MacLeod might well sing of Duntulm:

> Wherein waxen candles blaze, and wine is drunk right
> Freely, these from wan and gleaming cups of silver in
> A mansion wide and joyous and full of music.

However, while retaining the MacArthurs as hereditary pipers, the strains of other instruments were now heard in its halls: the *viol da gamba*, court music to accompany dancing lessons and even the sound of castanets! 

Despite the ties which bound them to Duntulm, it seems that the MacDonalds had never really lost their attachment to the district of Sleat. By the 1670s at least they had established a home at Armadale. Here they resided for just over 20 years until the house was fired upon by Government troops in 1690. This reprisal was for the part that Sir Donald played in Killiecrankie and his subsequent obdurate refusal to come to terms with the King. These were very difficult times for the MacDonalds, for on the death of the old Sir Donald in 1695, his son, Sir Donald, 4th Baronet, succeeded to an estate under threat of forfeiture and burdened with debts. For a time he lived in Glasgow and, shortly after removing to Frankfield, Culross, he was taken prisoner by the Government on suspicion of being a Jacobite. On his release in 1714 he returned to Duntulm although Armadale 'adorned

Plan of Duntulm.

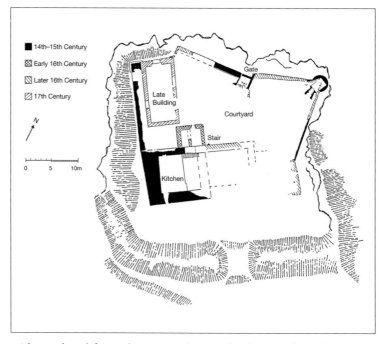

with stately edifices, pleasant gardens, and other regular policies' was retained. A great ball was held at Duntulm on the eve of the 1715 Rebellion in honour of those setting off to support the Stuart cause. In 1892 Charles Fraser-Mackintosh heard from an old woman of 103 years of age, that in her youth she had known an old woman called Mary MacDonald who had been under-chambermaid at Duntulm. This Mary had danced at this ball when Lord Lovat and other Highland nobility were guests at the castle. She also related that Mary had been married at the castle to either a Donald or Alexander MacDonald, a claim supported in a household account of 1732 which records payment to 'Mary McDond and the pipers . . .'

The failure of the 1715 Rebellion left Sir Donald a broken man and returning to Duntulm he died there in March 1718. The estate had been seized by the Crown but when it was eventually put up for sale in 1723, it was purchased by the creditors and restored to the MacDonalds in 1726. Just a year later the whole of the estate was erected by Crown Charter into a barony, the document setting out that possession of the 'Manor place of Duntulm' would suffice for possession of the whole estate. Yet while Duntulm remained in occupation no chief had resided there since the young Donald MacDonald, who died there unmarried in 1720. His successor as chief had been his uncle James, and shortly afterwards James' son, Alexander. Most of Alexander's early years were spent at Edinburgh and St. Andrews, although he does seem to have come to Duntulm in 1727 for a great ball held to celebrate the return of the estate to the MacDonald Chief. However, he does not appear to have taken up full residence, and the final record of activity before its desertion is an account for servants' wages up to Whitsunday, 1732.

Thereafter the empty shell was quarried to provide stone and timber for the new MacDonald residence then under construction at Monkstadt. Building accounts record the transportation of large quantities of stone by sea from Duntulm between 1732 and 1736, with the new building finally completed after lengthy delays in 1741.

Reasons for the abandonment of Duntulm are not hard to supply. In addition to its unsuitability for the 18th century lifestyle of a chief, it had probably stood in a state of disrepair during the time it lay in the hands of the Crown Commissioner. James MacDonald, who succeeded in 1720, could understandably have felt little attachment to the building, while his son and successor, Alexander, might equally be

Looking westwards across the western part of the site and towards Holm island, from the north tower. The sea-gate is visible to the right and the Late Building to the left.

forgiven for finding Duntulm a poor exchange for his former residences in the lowlands. As usual however, tradition furnishes an equal variety of much more colourful reasons for why the MacDonalds should quit their seat. One story relates how a nurse was cradling the chief's young son by the window overlooking the Minch, when the child wriggled from her grasp and fell to the rocks below. Thereafter the chief was said to have been unable to live in the building so strong was his grief. A second tradition tells of how the ghost of Donald Gorm Mor would frequently return with two companions to help themselves to the drink in the cellars and, by their appearance and noise, frighten away the earthly inhabitants of the castle. Eventually the advice of a saintly man was sought, whereupon the residents were told to get seven men together, each with a torch of burning bog-pine and that with these the ghosts could be driven out of the castle. Faced with these powerful charms, Donald and his companions were driven back, but not before Donald had exclaimed:

> if it were not for thy slender lance of fire
> This would have been to thy hurt young Donald Gorm.★

## DESCRIPTION

Nature could hardly have fashioned a situation more fitting for a castle than Duntulm. The great finger of olivine basalt which juts out into the Minch is fringed with irregular precipices falling 30m. to the sea below. The only approach is from the west where any unfriendly intent would have been plainly visible long before the castle was reached. In its heyday as the home of the MacDonald Chiefs it must have appeared a noble structure and symbol of both MacDonald strength and paternalism dominating a landscape dotted with homesteads. In 1772 when Moses Griffiths made a sketch of the castle for his companion, Thomas Pennant, its form was still apparent. More remarkable yet is the account of the castle by an old man who remembered when it was complete. He related that:

> The outline of the chief's galley is drawn upon the window
> of a room. The stair case is close by and was built outside the
> wall of the building, ascending what now looks a mere

★ As Donald Gorm Mor's nephew, Donald Gorm died in 1643, tradition would therefore have the castle abandoned almost a century before the actual event.

buttress over an arch-way, and leading to an upper chamber –
possibly communicating with all the chambers of that upper
storey. The two large windows now in ruins, one in the
former banqueting hall and one looking northwards over the
little bay, were lookout posts, a man was always stationed at
each and cannon protruded below. As already stated, at high
tide formerly the sea cut off the building from the mainland,
so that it was an island Castle; and the bridge which spanned
this arm of the ocean was raised every night and let down
only during the day in time of peace. The underground
rooms, now filled up, were lofty and spacious; while a wide
corridor ran between them, at the end of which lay the
dungeons. A vaulted room, which was under a tower that has
fallen within the last year, was the kitchen.

As late as the end of the 19th century, parts of the tower walls stood to
roof height, their rich decorative embellishments only able to provide
a glimpse of what has been lost over the centuries since its
abandonment. The castle was once a tight and ordered complex of
buildings enclosed by a stout curtain wall and angle turrets. Sadly, as a
result of neglect and quarrying stone for the MacDonald house of

MacGibbon and Ross's second view of
Duntulm shows the castle from the
south. At the time this was made the
tower was standing to its corbels, with
the base of a bartizan still plainly visible
at the angle. At the beginning of the
20th century this whole mass collapsed.

Monkstadt, it has become a disordered confusion of broken walls and fallen debris. Only in parts it is possible to recover something of the castle's former glory, the once 'Comelie House' where the Highland nobility were entertained for a week. Such lavish balls were held that they remained as a treasured jewel in the memory of a young under-chambermaid at the castle until her dying day as an old woman. Now debris fills the hollows and creates new ones that bear little relationship to the former layout; undoubtedly some of the basement rooms running off the 'wide corridor' described by one who remembered its layout, lie intact beneath the turf waiting to be revealed through careful excavation.

## THE DITCH

Across the neck of the headland lie the remains of the castle ditch, a wide cutting made into the bedrock which at either end terminates in a steep declivity. Though now largely filled with stone and debris fallen from the castle walls, sufficient remains suggest a causeway across the middle, wide enough to allow carts bringing in goods and provisions.

## THE TOWER

Beyond the ditch lies the tower, a large square building forming the south-west corner of the castle defences. The drawing made by Moses Griffiths in 1772 shows it virtually entire, and until the turn of the present century the south wall stood to gable height. From windows marked on the earlier drawings it appears to have had four floors, including a vaulted basement or undercroft. The tower was crowned with a steeply pitched gable roof, and projecting out from the south-west corner was an angle-tower ornamented with 'dog-tooth and nail-head' patterns. Only the undercroft now remains, approached by a steep flight of stone steps opening into the vaulted chamber lit by a single window in the south wall. A small recess in the north wall may have functioned as a cupboard, and at the south-east corner of the room there is a chimney tunnel now blocked in the vaulting. This is undoubtedly the kitchen described by the old man who remembered the castle when it was occupied. Originally it was entered from the north, although this doorway was blocked when the northern tower was built.

## THE NORTHERN TOWER

At a later date a second and smaller tower was built against the outside face of the north wall of the tower. Presumably an extension to the living space within the tower, it was not large, measuring only 3m. x 3.5m. internally. What it lacked in length and breadth it gained in height for it contained three floor levels, the uppermost lying within the eaves of its gabled roof.

The ground floor level was divided by a partition wall into two long narrow rooms. The eastern most room was lit by a window in the north wall, some of this light filtering through a wide arch in the partition into the room to the west. It was here that the MacDonald galley was etched out of the mortar. Unfortunately this section of

The vaulted basement of the tower; this for a time functioned as the kitchen.

walling has now fallen. This second room was otherwise windowless, and covered with a ceiling which sprang from the east wall to the partition.

The first-floor level above contained a fireplace within the north wall, its tunnel running up within the wall to a chimney set at the centre of the gable. A little over 2m. from the floor, the seating for timber joists which carried the floor of the room above are visible in the west wall of this tower. At the south-east corner of this later tower a substantial section of walling runs eastwards for some 5.5m. The remnants of once-projecting stone slabs indicate the position of an external staircase. This is almost certainly the one mentioned by the old man, for the buttress he mentions was part of the window of the north tower. The wall can be traced for a further 3m. to the point where it turns southwards then disappears. This would appear to represent the rear, northern, wall of a building shown on both the Moses Griffiths and Daniell illustrations; a two-storey building with a window indicated between the floors might suggest a stairway at this point lit at mid-height. In January 1990, the upper section of this tower fell away.

## THE CURTAIN WALL

A stout mortar-bonded stone wall enclosed the summit of the knoll. To the east and north the castle walls run in straight sections that angle sharply to allow only the minimum of space between the wall and the cliff edge. Along the western and southern sides the wall varies between 2 to 2.5m. in thickness, incorporating in its south-west angle the tower already described.

The only visible entrance is in the middle of the north wall where a steep descent between flanking passage walls leads out to a narrow ledge and cleft in the cliff face. The gateway passage lay beneath a small but disproportionately high tower. Immediately above the door opening, on the inner wall face is a tall recess within which the door or cullis could be raised. What little pictorial evidence exists indicates the approximate height of the tower within which the operating gear would have been housed. It is improbable that this was the only entrance unless large sections of the cliff edge have fallen away making it impossible to walk round the circuit. Daniell does in fact suggest

what could be an entrance through the wing built against the west face of the tower.

The earlier defensive arrangements covering the north and east faces of the castle comprised a substantial curtain with at least one drum tower at the north-east angle. This appears to have been lowered in the late 16th century to allow the modernisation of the defences in the era of the cannon. The small vaulted chamber within the drum is still accessible down a steep stone stair past the stone-checked doorway. It was almost certainly used as a subterranean magazine to serve a gun on the new platform overhead. The revision seems also to have affected the west and south walls to a lesser extent. Bartizans already existed on the outer angles of the tower and another, perhaps of the mid-16th century, was built at the north-west angle over the stump of the lowered north curtain. Unlike those on the tower this was of square plan. At the south-east angle an acute angle was given to part of the new curtain enabling artillery to play along the outer wall face. This too had an underground storeroom lit by a narrow slit. A short length of curtain running northwards from the north-east corner of the Late

Graffito of a ship, reputedly the MacDonald's birlinn, incised in the mortar next to the window shown in picture above. This fell away when the window arch collapsed (after J. MacDonald).

Building has small apertures for cannon or handguns, perhaps those referred to in the old man's reminiscences.

The overall design of the new curtain and artillery platforms owes much to contemporary practices throughout Europe and evolved from Italian and Spanish precedents using 'star' plans (the *trace italienne*). During the English Civil War most combatants became familiar with the sconces and siegeworks of the new warfare, however those at Duntulm are considerably earlier and lack that later refinement of re-entrant checks before dying back into the curtain.

## THE HALL

One of the latest buildings on the site lies within the north-eastern corner of the castle. This is a rectangular hall with walls 0.5m. in thickness enclosing an area some 10m. x 4.5m. It has doorways in both the west and east walls, and a window in the northern gable wall. A late date is indicated not only by its condition but also because it appears to overlay an already reduced curtain wall on its western side. The purpose of this building is uncertain but it may have been the banqueting hall recalled by an early observer.

# Dunvegan Castle
NG 2470 4906

DUIRINISH PARISH

ROUTE

Take the A863 from Sligachan or the A850 from Portree to Dunvegan.
Continue northwards past the village of Dunvegan for a kilometre.

HISTORY

Dunvegan Castle, home of the chiefs of the Clan MacLeod, is most
famous of all the castles in the Hebrides. In occupation by the same
family for over seven centuries, the castle is the longest continuously
occupied residence in Scotland. This is borne out by its architecture, a
succession of different structures accumulated over the centuries, and
compressed together into a single angular slab on the summit of a
basalt outcrop on the eastern shores of Loch Dunvegan.

Supposed appearance at the time of
Leod', by W. D. Simpson (*The Book of
Dunvegan,* Vol.I, xxx., 1938).

St. Clement's, Rodel, Isle of Harris. Built by Alasdair 'Crotach' MacLeod and where he is buried.

The early history of the site is unknown. The name Dun Bhegan points to an ancient origin, and has been interpreted as derived from the 'fort of Began' (a Scandinavian personal name occuring in Begansted – 'Began's homestead', in Iceland). Indeed, the situation alone would recommend itself for a fortification of Iron Age type, such as is found elsewhere around the coastline of Skye.

In the 12th century Skye was a Norwegian possession, overseen by the Kings of Man and the Isles. At this time it was administered by Sheriff Pal Balkeson, who held in his own right Sleat, Waternish, Trotternish and Snizort, as well as lands in Harris and North Uist. Loch Dunvegan was of old known as Loch Phallort (Loch of Pal).

The fort of Dunvegan, together with the whole of Duirinish, Bracadale, Minginish and a part of Trotternish was reputedly held by the MacRailds. By 1231 all these territories had passed into the hands of one man, Leod, eponymous founder of clan MacLeod. Tradition relates that Leod was a grandson of Godred the Black, King of Man and the Isles (1154–1187), and foster son of Pal Balkeson. It was as heir to Pal Balkeson and by a judicious marriage to the heiress of MacRaild that these extensive territories were consolidated within the one house. During Leod's chiefship momentous events were taking place in Northern Scotland, culminating in the Treaty of Perth in 1266. By

Alasdair's tomb, with his effigy lying within the niche. A masterpiece of West Highland sculpture.

this treaty the Kingdom of Man and the Isles passed to the Crown and Leod's feudal superior now became the Earl of Ross. It might be presumed that it was either Leod, or his successor Norman, who fixed upon Dunvegan as the chief residence of the clan, however the appearance of the castle during those early chiefships is far from clear. The first securely dated structural phase is the Fairy Tower, built in the time of Alasdair Crotach (1500–47). This was clearly preceded by two major, but not closely dateable, structural phases, the first being the curtain wall and sea-gate (?13th century), followed thereafter by the tower which is typologically of the 14th to 15th-century style.

Doubtless the remains of a succession of early timber or stone buildings lie buried within the defences. While tradition and the documentary record outline the early fortunes of the clan, with singular exceptions they reveal nothing of domestic life at the family seat. An apocryphal story is told of John, the 5th Chief, who was a ferocious man with an ungovernable temper. He tried to dissuade his daughters from marrying two brothers, sons of his vassal, and when reason failed, he had the brothers severely flogged before ordering them to be flung from the castle over the cliffs.

It is only from the 16th century that records and traditions began to reveal something of the life and events which took place within the

Effigy of *Alasdair Crotach MacLeod*
(*c.*1450–1547) over his tomb in St.
Clement's, Rodel, Harris (RCAHMS).

castle walls. Alasdair Crotach ('Hunchback') was not only a most able warrior but also a cultivated diplomat. His nickname arose from an axe wound received during a skirmish around 1480 that left him with a permanent deformity. Yet he could sit with ease at the King's table, where he was reputedly once goaded by a lesser-mannered nobleman, who foolishly enquired whether Skye could boast a roof so lofty, a table so laden, and candelabra so ornate as that then before them. Such a taunt to a warrior of Alasdair's standing might well have ended differently had the men not been guests of the King. However, the man was politely invited to come to Dunvegan and see for himself. Now after such insulting behaviour few men would place themselves in the hands of one they had so offended. Yet this man was clearly a fool – and besides which, the story demands it – he appeared one day at the castle gate. Expecting to be invited inside, he was led instead to the top of Healabhal Mór (MacLeod's Table). There, as the shadows of night stole across the sky, a line of clansmen rimmed the plateau, each holding aloft a blazing torch to illuminate the sumptuous feast spread before them. After the banquet Alasdair pointed to the star-studded sky and asked if this was not a more impressive roof, or the table before them of vaster extent? As to the candelabra, could anything be more precious than these faithful clansmen? Appropriately humbled, the nobleman apologised.

As patron of the arts, Alasdair is remembered in tradition as the chief who encouraged the famous pipers, the MacCrimmons, and endowed their piping college at Borreraig with a grant of the districts of both Borreraig and Galtrigil. His most enduring artistic legacy however is surely his own tomb, set within the south wall of St. Clement's at Rodel, Harris. Completed in 1528 some 18 years before his death in 1547, it is the supreme example of stone-carving in the Western Isles.

About the year 1540 Alasdair Crotach handed over the chiefship to his son, William, who in turn left as heir a daughter of about nine years of age. The problems now surrounding the question of succession consumed the MacLeods in a fierce struggle, both within the clan and against outside interests, who saw an opportunity to acquire some of the MacLeod territories. The wardship of the young heiress was a coveted prize, for by feudal law Mary was the rightful successor. The clan nevertheless determined to revert to the Gaelic law of kin-based succession, and Iain A'Chuil Bhain (Iain of the Fair Locks), a third

Dunvegan Castle from the east as depicted by Francis Grose in 1790. The Fairy Tower built by *Alasdair Crotach* is to the left and the derelict Tower to the right. Between is the new hall built by *Rory Mór* in 1623, with the 'great lummie' and balustrade added by *Iain Breac* in 1664. The stone buildings below the castle were built in 1734 as the Factor's Office and residence.

View of the castle from the south-east in 1772 by Moses Griffiths; on the left notice the wing added by *Iain Breac* in 1684.

cousin of Alasdair Crotach, was acclaimed chief. Before long, Donald, one of the sons of Alasdair, who had fled abroad and could not be traced when the succession was debated, returned to Skye. While his claim was greater than Iain's, the clan agreed to leave Iain in possession during his lifetime, but that thereafter it would revert to Donald and his heirs. This decision meant that Iain Dubh, son of Iain, would not succeed his father as chief. Iain however harboured covetous ambitions for the position, and by actions earning him the epithet Dubh (dark), brought the taint of murder within the walls of the chief residence. The clan now chose Iain Dubh's young nephew, Norman, as chief, and his brother, Donald Breac as Tutor. On their return to Dunvegan however, they were confronted at the sea-gate by Iain Dubh in full armour. The castle gate was slammed shut behind them, the portcullis dropped and they were put to death on the spot. Iain's usurpation was denounced

by the Crown, and Mary of Guise tried to raise a force to recover the
castle taken by 'wikkit Hielanmen'. Despite this royal rage, Iain
maintained his position, ever seeking a way to lay his hands on Alasdair
Crotach's younger son, Norman, and so secure the succession. Mary,
Alasdair's daughter, was nevertheless still regarded as rightful heir under
feudal law by the Crown. The Earl of Argyle saw Mary as a coveted
prize in strengthening his own position in the Isles, and sought to
marry her to one of his clansmen, a Campbell. A deputation of 11
Campbells arrived at the castle to discover whether Iain would be
prepared to give up his position in favour of Mary. Feigning a sympa-
thetic acquiescence, Iain invited them to a feast, where each Campbell
was tightly sandwiched between two of his own staunch men. When
the toast was called instead of ruby wine a cup of blood was placed
before each guest. At this signal the Campbells fell lifeless at the hands
of their table companions. Argyle now resorted to another ploy, namely
winning the favour of Norman, Alasdair Crotach's younger son, and
inducing the MacDonalds of Sleat to aid in supporting a restoration of
the succession to the proper line. In 1559 Norman appeared at the gate
of Dunvegan to claim his rights, and avenge himself on Iain Dubh for
the murder of his brother, Donald. Torquhil MacSween, warden of the
castle since the days of Norman's father, willingly opened the gates to
him, as Iain, realizing all was lost, fled. As a fugitive, first in Pabbay, then
Ireland, he quarrelled with the O'Donells who murdered him by the
fearsome method of thrusting hot irons through his bowels.

Until the succession of Sir Roderick MacLeod (Rory Mór) in
1595, the intervening generations of chiefs appear to have left little
visible mark on the castle. The final major conflict between the
MacLeods and MacDonalds was fought out at Coire na Creich in the
Cullin in 1601. In the reconciliation which followed the MacDonalds
came to Dunvegan Castle for a great feast. The carousing continued for
days with competitions held between bards, pipers, jesters and athletes.
Great quantities of wine were consumed in the halls, so that:

> twenty times drunk we were each day,
> Nor did we rebel against it any more than he

It is easy to see how Rory Mór could easily exceed the annual ration
of 4 tuns of wine imposed on him by the King because of 'the great
and extraordinary excess of drinking commonly used among the

Dunvegan Castle.

commons and tenants of the Isles'. In 1625 alone his debt for wine was £509, it is appropriate that two of the castle treasures acquired during his chiefship should be the Dunvegan Cup and the great drinking horn holding over a litre which, on coming of age, each heir must drain of claret at a single draught!

From being a remote and often troublesome insular possession of the Scottish Crown, by Rory Mór's day the influence of central authority had largely tamed the Island chiefs. Now drawn to play a role on a national rather than insular state, both MacLeods and MacDonalds were travelling more widely around the kingdom and abroad. They were subjected to influences which profoundly affected their tastes, and introduced into Dunvegan Castle elements startlingly at variance with the traditional West Highland style. But one example is the magnificent oak sideboard which stands in the dining room. This was said to have been transported by Rory Mór all the way from London in 1616. The very building it occupies is another. Built by Rory Mór in 1623, its form and proportion, relative lightness of construction and generous window provision mark a watershed in the architecture of a chiefly residence. In the 17th century the 'stark strenthie castillis' of necessity were superceded by structures of relative comfort which also commanded the respect and approbation of visiting peers in the matter of taste.

Little appears to have been done to the castle by Iain Mór, Rory's

Building inscription recording the repairs carried out by *Iain Breac* in 1686. The text reads: 'John MacLeod, Lord of Dunvegan, Chief of his Clan, Lord Baron of Duirinish, Harris, Waternish, etc, joined in the bond of Matrimony to Flora MacDonald, restored this tower, by far the most ancient part of the habitation of his ancestors for long fallen into ruin, in the year 1686.'

son and successor as chief in 1626. Indeed the financial obligations he contracted during his tenure marked the start of the difficulties later to assail the family, and may well have prohibited any major rebuilding at this time. On the death of Iain in 1649, his son, Rory Mir (the Witty) became chief. As Rory was only 14 years of age his uncle, Roderick of Talisker, was appointed Tutor or guardian. In the struggle between the King and Oliver Cromwell, Roderick brought the MacLeods out in support of the King. By July 1654, however, the Royalist cause in Scotland had been signally lost to the Cromwellian forces under General Monck. The defeated Royalist generals passed the winter of 1654–55 in Dunvegan's hospitable halls before escaping to the continent.

By 1656 Rory Mir had come of age and the services of his uncle Roderick were no longer required. Variously described as 'a man of uncommon livliness and wit', and a 'prodigal vitious spendthrift', either would explain how eight years of high living in the cities of Southern England could further deplete the family patrimony. On his death at the age of 28 years, his brother, Iain Breac succeeded to an estate crippled with debt. Ignoring the call to become embroiled in the struggle to restore the Stuart monarchy, Iain set to a path that would rebuild the family finances rather than reduce it still further. The trade in black cattle was a growing source of income, and with an increase in prosperity the castle was refurbished. While Iain was content as chief to shun travel outside his estates he was far from insensitive to current fashions. In 1664–65 he replaced the embrasures of his grandfather's building with a balustrade in fine Renaissance style. Just 20 years later he added a new wing to the west of the Fairy Tower, at the same time restoring the tower which had apparently stood uninhabited and in a state of disrepair. This work was subsequently commemorated by an inscription now built into the basement corridor.

Iain's purposeful policy to distance the MacLeods from the political upheavals, which had so drained its resources, served the clan well. The arts, as represented by piping, the harp, storytelling and song, flourished as never before. Dunvegan's halls proudly rang with the pibrochs of Padruig Og MacCrimmon and the lilting strains of Rory Morrison, the Blind Harper – or the poetic genius of Mairi N'in Alasdair Ruaidh (Mary MacLeod) and the wit of Iain's jester, Tormod MacHandy. This brief golden age, the final flowering of a mediaeval chiefdom, was carried out largely in a state of self-imposed isolation from the world beyond. Yet while candles were shining brightly in Dunvegan's halls, outside the nation was moving inexorably through political and religious crisis towards the events of 1715 and 1745.

## DESCRIPTION

The castle occupies the summit of a basalt outcrop rising some 15m. above the beach, and separated from the landward mass by a broad ditch. The platform on which the castle sits is an irregular oval of 1,500 square metres, around which the ground falls away steeply on all but the north-western side. Here a slack in the cliff offers a more gentle approach, with a doubly-curved flight of steps rising to the sea-gate.

## THE CURTAIN WALL AND SEA-GATE

With the possible exception of the ditch, the curtain wall with its sea-gate remains the only visible element of the 13th century castle occupied by Leod and his successor Norman. Constructed of partially coursed basalt rubble bonded with lime-mortar, it is 2m. in thickness and formerly rose to a corbelled parapet at a height of 3m. Originally the curtain wall completely encircled the platform, hugging its edge and protecting the early stone and timber buildings that lay within. These remains now lie buried within the courtyard, or overlain by the

Alexander Runciman's view of the castle in 1790 (National Galleries of Scotland).

Plan of the castle showing building work up to the close of the 17th century. The upper plan shows the hall of Rory Mór between the tower and Fairy Tower. The west wing added to the Fairy Tower is that built by Iain Breac in 1686.

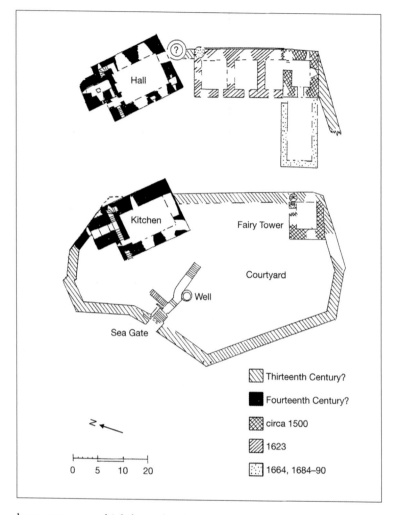

Hall

Kitchen

Fairy Tower

Courtyard

Well

Sea Gate

Thirteenth Century?

Fourteenth Century?

circa 1500

1623

1664, 1684–90

N

0   5   10   20

later structures which have absorbed or replaced the curtain wall on its eastern side.

To the north-west the curtain wall is breached by the sea-gate. Until an entrance was built on the landward side in 1748 this was the only entrance to the castle; its position is reminiscent of the gate in the north wall of Duntulm Castle. It is approached by a winding flight of steps up the slack, or break in the basalt stack. Entrance through the curtain wall was through a wide doorway covered by a roughly pointed voussoir arch. In the 16th century the width of the gate was reduced, and its height lowered by the insertion of a decorated lintel slab. Beyond the door which is now represented by an iron 'yett' or grille is the short vaulted passage where in 1557 Iain Dubh reputedly murdered his brother and nephews. At the end of this passage are the slots in the side-walls for a portcullis operated from a timber cradle above. Beyond, a flight of steps rise between cheek-walls to a second gate; the bar-hole for the timber which secured it is plainly visible in the north wall. Thereafter the steps divide. One flight leads northwards towards the original tower entrance, the other continues eastwards, rising up to the courtyard level. Midway in its ascent there is a small doorway giving access to the well. At the baptism of Norman, the 25th Chief, in 1812, one of the clansmen, 'who had testified his loyal joy by mixing something stronger with its water', tumbled into this well and was drowned. As no one noticed a discrepancy between the numbers arriving and leaving, the mishap was only revealed much later when the water developed a peculiar taste!

## THE TOWER

Sometime in the 14th century a large tower was erected at the north-eastern end of the platform. Rising from massive basement walls 3m. in thickness to a height of four storeys, its construction involved the demolition of part of the defences, and a realignment of a short stretch of curtain wall to the north. Like so much of the castle, it has subsequently been substantially modified. The major alterations date from the 1790s when Norman, the 25th Chief, re-roofed the structure and made it habitable.

## THE BASEMENT

Initially the basement appears to have been used as a store-room. It was lit by narrow loops, one of which remains visible in the east wall, though these were partially blocked by the later insertion of vaulting. Subsequently it became the kitchen and a large fireplace was cut into the south wall. Today we see it divided by a partition, and it is no longer easy to visualize the claustrophobic heat and noisy bustle that must have taken place here in preparation for the lavish banquets held in the room above. From here an endless stream of kitchen staff would transport brimming dishes up the narrow stairway, set within the thickness of the north wall, which opened out into the Great Hall.

## THE GREAT HALL

Now the drawing room, there is little in its rather studied elegance to accord with a 17th century bard's description of 'a large wine-hall and a numerous host', a roaring fire in the north wall, and blazing torches around the walls. This room also witnessed much darker deeds, as when the 11 eleven Campbells invited to feast with Iain Dubh were violently slaughtered as they sat here at the table.

The hall was entered from the courtyard level by a door at the head of a short stair the north end of the west wall. From here a flight of stairs led upwards within the thickness of the wall to the hall. The only other original feature of note in this room is the vaulted mural guard-chamber which lies at the south-west angle.

## SECOND AND THIRD FLOORS

Access to the floors above was formerly by means of stairs set within the thickness of the east wall. Now private apartments, they have been so altered as to show no ancient features.

## THE JAMB

Jutting out from the north face of the keep is a subsidiary tower or 'jamb'. It is entered from the head of the stairs, where a trap-door in the ceiling discloses a *meutriere*, or 'murder-hole' through which stones and missiles could be dropped on any attackers who penetrated the doorway. From here a short flight of stairs leads into a small vaulted chamber with a garderobe in the north-east corner. A flagstone inset with an iron ring was formerly the only access to a basement prison cell. Sometime in the 16th century a door was cut through the north wall to the basement. This was probably made to allow provisions to be brought into the castle more easily, for another opening was made to the middle landing of the stairs linking the Great Hall and kitchen.

Later 18th-century illustrations show the jamb to have stood no higher than the tower. Today stairs rise from a second small chamber with loop-holes and garderobe in the north wall, within a jamb carried in the 1840s to the extravagant height of almost 40m!

## THE FAIRY TOWER

The small tower at the south-eastern corner of the castle is said to have been the work of Alasdair Crotach, the 8th Chief, who died in 1547. It was built to incorporate the curtain wall and the remains of the parapet corbels are clearly visible in the outer walls.

The tower has three floors, with access originally by a steep newel stair within the wall at the north-eastern corner. It was in the room on the second floor where Johnson slept on his 64th birthday, lulled by the cascading waters of Rory Mór's nurse, a small waterfall outside his window. Sir Walter Scott also slept here in August 1814, by which time the room was said to be haunted by the ghost of Rory Mór. Nevertheless, after a bottle of claret, '... without troubling myself about the ghost of Rorie More or anyone of his long line I went to bed and slept quietly till my servant called me in the morning'.

At the head of the newel stair a short straight staircase opens out onto the parapet. Its embrasures, with weep-holes and projecting stone runnels, originally encircled a central garret. In the early 19th century the northern section was suppressed when the adjacent wing was heightened. Undoubtedly the most wilful act of vandalism carried out on the castle in all the seven centuries of its history occurred when the Fairy Tower was absorbed with a bland wall-face. At a stroke the harmonious and picturesque irregularity of a mediaeval stronghold was transformed into a slab of 19th-century Scottish baronial architecture.

The Fairy Tower, now absorbed within later works, shown in a later-19th-century sketch by D. MacGibbon and T. Ross.

## THE NEW HALL

In 1623 a building was raised between the tower and the Fairy Tower which marked a radical departure from the mediaeval style. It was built for Rory Mór who had been encouraged by what he had seen in his travels to build a spacious and elegant residence that was at the same time fashionable. Its dimensions (16m. x 8m.) and proportions compare favourably with the later rectangular buildings at Caisteal Camus, and Dun Sgathaich, indicating a trend not confined to the MacLeods alone.

The building consisted of three floors and a garret. The latter was replaced in the early 19th century by a fourth floor and a flat roof. The basement contains three unvaulted cellars, presumably used for stores and domestic services. Access is now by a corridor running along the western side of the building.

The floor above contained the hall, which was entered from the courtyard, presumably by a flight of steps. All trace of these disappeared in the 19th century when the original west wall above the basement level was demolished, and in the remodelling built out further to the west. In a drawing of 1790 no windows are evident in the east wall, which rises two floors to an embrasured parapet resting on a corbelled table. Set behind this parapet is the third floor lit by windows and originally covered with a steeply pitched roof containing the garret.

Under the directions of Iain Breac, in 1664 the embrasured parapet was replaced by a balcony of Italianate design, terminating at its northern end in a small turret with a conical cap. A massive and ponderous stepped chimney was raised from third floor level to over-top the roof-ridge. The fireplace lintel is in all probability the one now set in the wall above the porch, which carries the arms of Iain Breac impaled with those of his wife, Flora MacDonald of Sleat.

## THE SOUTH WING

Twenty years later in 1684–86, Iain Breac added a wing of his own to the west of the Fairy Tower. Three storeys in height with a garret in the roof, only the kitchen in the basement survives in its original form.

Thereafter, such minor changes were made to ease the building into becoming a more comfortable residence for its later inhabitants.

Dunvegan Castle in a late 19th-century view from the north.

# Eilean Donan

NG 8851 2581

KINTAIL PARISH

ROUTE

In its route north towards the Kyle of Lochalsh the A85 (T) follows the eastern edge of Loch Duich from its head to the village of Dornie at its mouth. The castle lies to the west of the road just before reaching Dornie. Times of opening are given on the signboard.

HISTORY

When defence was a consideration in the siting of early settlements the small tidal island at the mouth of this loch would have been an obvious attraction. Until the 1920s the remains of an Iron Age fort were visible on the landward side of the island. Its outer defensive wall was vitrified, the result of a technique of construction which consisted of raising the stonework with timber throughout and then setting fire to the woodwork. Extremely high temperatures were reached within the wall, causing the stone to melt and fuse into a solid mass.

The island takes its name from the 6th-century Irish saint, Bishop

The 'new' castle at *Eilean Donan* from the north-west.

The 1920s construction upon the earlier fabric, from the south.

Donan, who came to Scotland around AD 580 and found martyrdom together with 56 of his fellow monks on the Isle of Eigg. Along this part of the western coastline churches dedicated to the saint are recorded for Loch Carron, Loch Broom, and at Kildonan on Skye. It is quite probable that an early Christian cell was established here on the island sometime during the late 6th or 7th century AD.

The exuberance of the Gaelic imagination rarely suffers the doubts which bedevil the diligent historian and will often supply a more rounded explanation than that dependent on fragmentary evidence. So it is that an old tale in the District traces the origin of the name not from the late 6th-century wandering saint but to the colony of otters that for generations have inhabited its shores. Cu-Donn (Brown Dog) is Gaelic for the otter and it was widely held that the King of the Otters could be clearly recognised by its coat of pure silver and white. The story has it that the King of the Otters died and his glittering robe of silver was buried on the island beneath the foundations of the castle.

Another story has the castle built early in the 13th century during the reign of Alexander II as a measure of defence against the Scandinavians. However, its early history is far from clear. It has been claimed that in the 13th century Alexander II sent an expedition to the Isles amongst whom there was an Irishman named Cailean Fitzgerald. Cailean was said to be under the patronage of Walter Stewart, Earl of Menteith, and to have been granted government of the castle. The original charter setting out the grant of Kintail to Cailean as a barony no longer exists, but from what is known of it in redact, it may have been a forgery. Far more colourful is the mythical tale of the castle's origin arising indirectly from the conflict between a wealthy chief said to be of the race of the Mathesons, and his son. As an infant the son had received his first drink from a raven's skull and this had given him the power to understand the language of the birds. As a youth he went to Rome to study and became a great linguist. One day his father asked him to explain what the birds were saying and was told that they were talking about how one day his father would be waiting upon his son like a servant. This so angered his father that the son was turned

*Eilean Donan* as depicted in the *Saturday Magazine* of 1835. The engraver has had difficulty in interpreting the view reproduced by Daniell in 1819. He has, however, clearly indicated the door and two of the openings in the hexagonal bastion.

out of the house to make his way in the world. Eventually he landed on the shores of France only to hear that the King there was greatly annoyed by the chirping of birds around the palace. The boy set off to offer his help in getting rid of them and soon discovered that the cause was a noisy dispute among the birds, which, together with the King, he was able to resolve. The King was so pleased that peace and quiet had been restored that he presented the boy with a fully-manned ship. This took the boy to many distant lands. On one of his voyages he was invited by the ruler of a far-off country to dine at his palace. On arriving he found the place so overrun with rats that they even invaded the dining table during the meal. The next evening the boy returned to the castle with a cat under his coat and when the rats gathered around the table he let it loose amongst them. The King was so pleased that he offered a hogshead of gold for the cat. After an absence of ten years the young man returned to Kintail and his ship anchored at Totaig. The sight of such a royal vessel caused a considerable stir in the district and all wondered who the richly dressed wealthy young man might be. Arriving at his father's door, no one recognised him and he was received with great hospitality. His father set him at the table and waited upon the young stranger himself, thereby fulfilling the prophesy of the birds. The son revealed who he was, proving his identity by a

An obviously 'well-heeled' visitor arrives safely, courtesy of the Dornie Ferry, on the west shore of Loch Long. But does he notice the remarkable building work taking place around the old castle?

birthmark on his shoulders and the father was reconciled to the boy whom he acknowledged as his heir. His son's abilities and knowledge of the world brought him into the favour of Alexander II who commissioned him to build Eilean Donan and protect his subjects against the Norwegians.

By the later 13th century the castle was in the hands of Kenneth MacKenzie, possibly a nephew of William, Third Earl of Ross, whose family, during the 13th and 14th centuries, were the superiors of Kintail. After the treaty of Perth in 1266, by which the Scandinavian territories were seceded to the Scottish Crown, Earl William laid claim to the Western Isles which both he and his father had subdued on behalf of the King. No doubt to curtail the rapidly growing power of Kenneth, his kinsman in Eilean Donan, William demanded that Kenneth resign the castle to him. Kenneth naturally refused whereupon the Earl of Ross led a large force against him. Supported by the old established clans of MacIver, MacAuley, Macbollan, and Tarlich, Kenneth inflicted a crushing defeat on the Earl of Ross's force. William was planning a second assault when he died in 1274, and his son Hugh failed to put this into effect. In 1304 Kenneth died and was buried on Iona. By this time the King had settled the barony of Kintail on Clan MacKenzie. It is claimed that in his wanderings Robert the Bruce was given shelter at Eilean Donan by Kenneth's successor who assisted him in his struggle against the English.

In 1331 Randolph, Earl of Moray and Warden of all Scotland, paid a visit to the castle and had sent a Crown Officer to prepare it for his arrival. Knowing the Earl to be a strict disciplinarian whose rigorous execution of the law was both well known and feared, fifty miscreants were executed and their heads placed on the wall of the castle to greet him as he sailed up the loch. The Earl was greatly pleased and claimed that the sight of justice so displayed was sweeter to him than any garland of roses.

By 1350 the Earl of Ross had signed a charter at Eilean Donan, from which it has been inferred that the strength of the MacKenzies was by now at low ebb. The Earl of Ross had made an attack on MacKenzie territory in Kinlochewe and Kenneth MacKenzie had pursued the raiders to recover his property with the loss of life of some of the Earl's men. The Earl of Ross succeeded in having Kenneth executed in Inverness and fear for the MacKenzie line was now so great that his heir Murdo MacKenzie was hastily sent to the Western

The castle from the east in 1885 (reproduced with permission from the George Washington Wilson Collection in Aberdeen University, B2066).

Isles and put under the protection of MacLeod of Lewis. In 1362 Murdo obtained a charter from David II confirming his title to the lands of Kintail. By this time the clan MacRae had settled in the district, moving here from the Beauly Firth, and they soon became the 'Mackenzie's Coat of Mail' defending and protecting the MacKenzie chiefs. They were joined shortly afterwards by the clan MacLennan and both clans greatly distinguished themselves under the Earls of Ross. By 1427, Euphemia, Countess of Ross, had survived two husbands and now had her eye on Alexander MacKenzie, the young Laird of Kintail. He was an extremely intelligent and handsome youth and the power of his House had grown considerably over the previous decades. Euphemia, now in her 40th year, is said to have been unsuccessful in proposing marriage to Alexander and held him prisoner until he reconsidered. By some means the Countess managed to lay hold of Alexander's gold signet ring. Knowing that Duncan MacAuley, Constable of Eilean Donan, had orders never to let in a stranger or to leave his post in the family's absence except without the ring as a token, Euphemia used this to lure MacAuley to Dingwall where his chief was being held. MacAuley was nevertheless suspicious and rather than entering the castle straight away he felt it prudent to make enquiries. As a result he discovered his chief was being held prisoner. Somehow MacAuley succeeded in communicating with Alexander and the pair determined that the only way to recover the situation was for MacAuley to seize the Countess's first cousin, Sir Walter Ross of Balnagown. Euphemia had by this time put a garrison of her own in Eilean Donan but a local force was soon raised, set off for the east coast and succeeded in seizing Sir Walter. Lord Lovat, the King's Lieutenant, heard of the kidnapping and set off to intercept MacAuley. Wisely the prisoner had been sent ahead and when Lovat caught up with MacAuley there ensued the battle thereafter known as Bealach nan Brog (the Pass of the Shoes). The name arose because some MacKenzies were travelling so light that they had to resort to tying their brogues against their chests to give them some protection against the enemies' arrows. A great many men on both sides died in the conflict but MacAuley's force won the day. They continued on their way unmolested until, just five miles from Eilean Donan, they met up with a gang of 30 men sent by the Countess to take grain to her garrison in the castle. The men were promptly seized and MacAuley's men took their place. Once admitted they overpowered the surprised garrison and now, with both trump cards in his possession, MacAuley was able to exchange his prisoners for the young laird. Subsequently the Countess retired to the abbey of Elcho and before long the power of the House of Ross was irrecoverably broken, with the Lords of the Isles now laying claim to their titles and possessions.

In 1497 Kenneth Oig MacKenzie died and, as his son John was a minor, management of the clan was invested in his uncle, Hector Roy MacKenzie, progenitor of the House of Gairloch. Hector did not discharge his obligations well. The clan became involved in feuds with other clans and Hector seems to have come into conflict with the Crown. It was becoming increasingly clear that Hector had little intention of relinquishing his position to that of the rightful heir, and John had to resort to the law to secure his patrimony. This was acknowledged on the 7th April 1511 when Hector was summoned to appear before the court for 'The wrongous intromitting, uptaking, and withholding [from John] of the mails fermez, profits and duties of all . . . the Lands of Kintail . . . and for the masterful holding of the said John MacKenzie of his house and castle of Eleandonain'. These were troubled times for the clan chiefs in the West for the Crown was gradually extending its authority over the chiefs. In 1503, Alexander

Gordon, Earl of Huntly, undertook to reduce Eilean Donan on behalf of the Crown, 'for the daunting of the Isles'. King James IV offered to provide ships and artillery and during an insurrection which broke out in 1504 the castle was occupied by the Earl. However, some of the garrison were lured outside the walls, and promptly despatched. Only a decade later of John of Kintail was to host James V at the castle during a northern tour.

The King's apprehension as to the highly charged atmosphere between the clans was well founded. The MacKenzies, together with the MacLeods of Dunvegan, disputed the claims of Donald Gorm MacDonald to the Lordship of the Isles. In 1539 Donald responded by sailing with the fleet of 50 galleys to Applecross and there laid waste the MacKenzie territories of Torridon and Kinlochewe. Donald then ordered his fleet to Eilean Donan as he had received a report that the castle was only lightly garrisoned. Indeed the only men in the castle at that time were its Constable, John Dubh Matheson, and a watchman. The only other person in the vicinity as the MacDonald forces were bearing down on the castle was Duncan MacGillechriosd (MacRae) and, seeing the plight of those in the castle, he hastened to their aid. The MacDonald forces battered at the door without effect and soon resorted to firing arrows at the windows. One killed Constable John Matheson, leaving only Duncan and the watchman to hold the castle. The besieged pair began to run short of ammunition and soon Duncan had only one arrow left which he resolved to keep until the opportunity arose for a good shot at the enemy. Meanwhile, sensing victory, Donald Gorm MacDonald sent his men to fetch a mast from one of the ships to use as a battering ram. As MacDonald was walking close to the castle walls looking for a point of weakness, Duncan drew his bow and fired his last arrow which pierced Donald in the foot. Rather than wait for a physician MacDonald impatiently wrenched it out. The barbs however severed an artery and nothing could be done to staunch the flow. Abandoning the siege the MacDonalds carried their chief to a little island opposite Ardintoul where he died, there-after named Larach Thig Mhic Domhnuil ('the site of the Mac-Donald's house'). His men returned in an attempt to set fire to the castle. They achieved only limited success before returning to their boats with the body of their chief. In return for his almost single-handed defence of the castle, Duncan had hopes of receiving the now-vacant post of Constable as a reward. The Lord of Kintail apparently

The castle from the south in the late 19th century (RCAHMS).

thought otherwise. In pique, at what he saw as Kintail's ingratitude, Duncan left the district having first married the widow of the former Constable, John Dubh Matheson. Within two years all of those who had taken part in the siege received a pardon from the King, James V.

In 1618 the vicarage of Kintail fell vacant on the death of Murdo Murchison also at the time Constable to Eilean Donan castle. The Reverend Mr. Farquhar was appointed to fill his place in both posts and for many years he lived in the castle in an 'opulent and flourishing condition, much given to hospitality and charity'. Occasionally he was visited by Colin, Earl of Seaforth, and his retinue of 'never less than three, and sometimes 500, men'. Mr. Farquhar was at first bound to furnish them with food for the first two meals and during Seaforth's stay many of the neighbouring chiefs would come to pay their respects, and to feast and drink in the halls of the castle. Colin, Earl of Seaforth, died in 1633. Mr. Farquhar's rights to both offices, together with the wadset rights to certain lands in Kintail were confirmed by his successor. Apparently the new Earl thought well of him for, in 1641, he placed his son George in his care where he remained for several years. Some ten years later however, he appears to have incurred the displeasure of the Earl's brother, Simon MacKenzie of Lochslin. A band of men had been raised to support Charles II and Lochslin was the leader of the group. However he refused to set off until Mr.

Farquhar had been moved from Eilean Donan. Mr. Farquhar quite rightly refused to leave, 'without violence, lest his going voluntarily might be interpreted as an abdication of his right'. At first none would support Lochslin and the young laird refused to condone any action against his foster-father. Eventually one George MacKenzie of Tarbet became so frustrated by the situation that he escorted Mr. Farquhar to the gate where Farquhar told him he would go without further trouble for he was 'well pleased to be rid of the island, because it was a bad habitation for a man of his age and corpulence'. The question of Mr. Farquhar's expulsion came before the Presbytery at Dingwall in 1661 but the collapse of the Royalist forces at Worcester resulted in the case not being heard.

After the execution of Charles I, George, Earl of Seaforth, was inspired to support the Royalist cause. In the final year of Mr. Farquhar's tenure the Scottish Parliament was sufficiently concerned about the situation in the West to impose a garrison on the castle. The soldiers treated the locals with great insolence and, as winter approached, they demanded that the people supply them with timber for fuel. A party of about thirty soldiers led by John Campbell and his Sergeant, Blythman, set off to enforce their demands on the Chamberlain at Inverinate. The soldiers were met by a deputation of ten men sent to complain about this imposition and, when the debate became heated, Campbell ordered the soldiers to fire their guns. This they did, fortunately without hurting any of the local men. However, seeing that Campbell was obdurate, the local men drew their swords and fell upon the soldiers. Campbell was struck a fierce blow which 'cut off his head, neck, right arm and shoulder from the rest of his body'. Blythman was killed crossing a stream thereafter known as 'Blythman's Ford'. Several other soldiers were killed and the rest put to flight. Needless to say, the garrison made no further demands for fuel and shortly afterwards withdrew from the castle. In 1654 retribution of a sort occurred when Cromwell's Lieutenant, General Monck, arrived in Kintail with an army which, doubtless, had already heard of the earlier incident. The district was plundered with many houses and huts burnt, cattle reived, and one Kintail man killed by the soldiers.

During the rising of 1715, the castle was again garrisoned by Government troops but was recovered by the men of Kintail on the eve of Sheriffmuir. Stuart supporters now gathered at the castle and a dance was held on the castle roof before they set out for their defeat, the aftermath of which left 58 widows in Kintail.

In 1719, a remarkably foolhardy plot was hatched to recover the mishap of 1715. The plan was to land a force of 300 Spanish soldiers on the west coast of Scotland to unite with the Highland forces and then march on Inverness. Despite much quarrelling between those in charge of the campaign, the Spanish force eventually disembarked in Eilean Donan and established a magazine in the low building at the rear of the castle, and to the west of the building by the entrance which was then in use as a manse. It was intended to push on rapidly to meet with the Highland force but the Government had received intelligence of the plan and at the same time a force set out from Inverness to intercept the rebels. Three Government ships patrolling the West Coast sailed into the loch and early on the morning of the 10th May 1719 two of these, the *Worcester* and the *Enterprise*, hove to by the castle which was garrisoned by 46 Spaniards. The castle was not built to withstand the firepower of such vessels and was soon reduced to ruins. Captain Herdman of the *Enterprise* was sent ashore to set fire to the powder magazine which exploded taking much of the castle with it, forcing those within to retreat inland. Here they were met by the Government forces from Inverness and, forced to make a stand, were decisively beaten in the pass of Glenshiel. Captain Boyle of the *Worcester* was able to report smugly to his master that Eilean Donan had been blown into ruins 'so that traitors might have one haunt the less to plot mischief against the King and the Laws'.

For two hundred years the castle stood derelict until something of its former appearance was resurrected on the site between 1912 and 1932 by Lt. Colonel MacRae-Gilstrap. The castle was picturesquely restored by Farquhar MacRae of Auchtertyre, to whom its 'original' appearance was said to have been revealed in a dream.

## DESCRIPTION

To the casual reader the following description of Eilean Donan may seem more detailed than that of the other castles. It has proved the most complex of any dealt with so far, and its description depends upon a more painstaking consideration of sources which preserve detailed information on features that no longer survive, or have been overlooked by previous writers.

Plan of *Eilean Donan*. Later tipping has obscured parts of the line of the early circuit as can be clearly seen by comparing the present topography with that shown on 19th-century photographs.

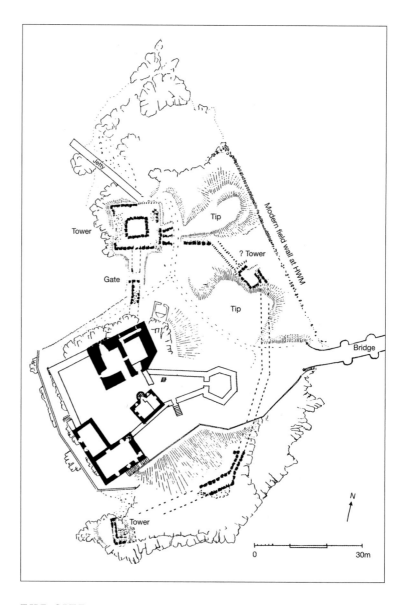

## THE SITE

The castle is built over the larger part of a small tidal island of pre-Cambrian Lewisian Gneiss. A low plateau of rock at the south-west corner falls steeply into the sea at the west and south. Beyond its steep landward faces the surface slopes gently in a series of rocky undulations to north and east. A small inlet at the south-west and a rough boulder-strewn beach at the north-west offer landing places to small craft.

## THE IRON AGE

No trace now remains of the Iron Age vitrified fort which was almost certainly perched on the higher southern outcrop except the detached fragments of its wall lying in the rough grass east of the tower.

## THE CELL OF ST. DONAN

Of the early ecclesiastical cell of St. Donan known to have been on the site not a trace remains.

## THE CASTLE
*First Phase, the Early Mediaeval Castle*

For some inexplicable reason, previous writers, including MacGibbon and Ross, have ignored the early castle, traces of which are still plainly evident to the most casual observer. Despite its being largely overlaid by builder's rubble from the recent rebuilding, the northern half of Eilean Donan retains the footings of towers and curtain walling probably used as a quarry by masons engaged in erecting the curtain round the newer and smaller courtyard on the higher outcrop. Outside the south and east of this new curtain lie further remains of the circuit of wall and towers.

This wall of enciente encloses an area of approximately 3,000 square metres, which is well over three-quarters of the land surface of the island. A major defensive feature of this circuit is a tower, represented by massive footings, at its northern extremity. Walls 4.3m. in thickness enclose what may have been a vaulted basement, 4m. x 5m. To the south the curtain runs out towards the southern outcrop, and 6m. from this tower the wall is pierced by a gateway 2.3m. wide, opening virtually on the high-tide mark. Eastwards the curtain runs 18m. before being angled south-east to continue 10m. to meet what appears to have been another rectangular tower. These footings have walls 1.8m. in thickness enclosing a floor area 3m. x 5m. Southwards the continuation of the curtain is obscured. It seems to have extended to meet a short stretch of robbed-out wall visible at the south-eastern extremity of the island. This wall appears to have run south-westwards

The slight but evident traces of a circuit wall and structures suggests the form of the first phase castle. A sea-gate appears to have been situated between the northern tower and the tower, the latter being the only element to persist through all subsequent changes.

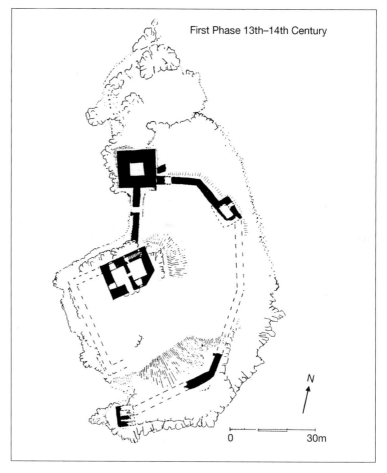

First Phase 13th–14th Century

0    30m

to the footings of another structure similar in size to that south-east of the north tower. This structure may also have been a tower erected on the knoll overlooking a small inlet. The remainder of the circuit lies beneath the walls of the present, and smaller, castle.

The nearest major castle to Eilean Donan is that of Urquhart on Loch Ness where similar topographical features and historical influences have resulted in surprising coincidence. Both sites have their prehistoric circuit on an outcrop at the south end of the site. The later works from the 13th century extend their enclosures on the lower ground to the north. In both cases, despite their different building periods, a substantial tower is sited on the water's edge overlooked by their upper courtyards. Only at Eilean Donan has the arrangement been altered by the suppression of the 'low' tower in favour of the dominant one on the higher outcrop (this higher tower is described in detail below). That this tower stood within the lifetime of the earlier, more extensive, defences is plainly apparent from a survey made in 1714 which shows the curtain of the smaller courtyard uncomfortably abutting the higher tower so that it partially obscures a window.

*The Second Phase*

The First Phase defences which encircled much of the island were in being throughout the 13th and most of, if not the whole, 14th century. After that date, for reasons unrecorded, the decision was taken to reduce the castle defences to enclose an area of 24m. x 22m., only 16 per cent of its former extent. It is difficult to reconcile the decision to shrink the defensive circuit on Eilean Donan with the fragmentary historical record. Certainly the extended circuit would have required a

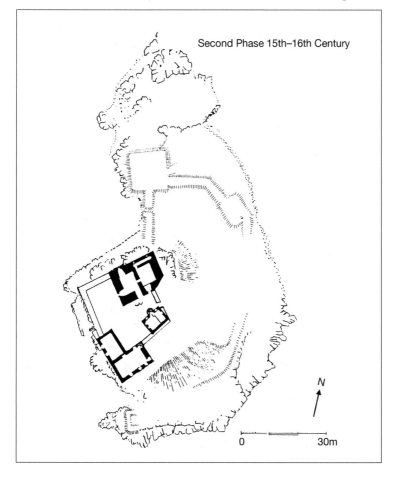

In its second phase the castle area contracted to occupy the low plateau at the south-west of the island. The tower became the focus of a much-reduced courtyard enclosure with buildings later erected along the southern curtain.

Second Phase 15th–16th Century

N

0          30m

far larger garrison than this later reduction. The most obvious drawback of this contraction was that the northern end of the island subsequently offered a foothold for an attacking party. In addition this uneven ground provided the attacker with some cover. No ditch was constructed around the new defences and the elevated position on the rock as well as the proximity of the sea to the west must have been thought adequate. In the Third Phase during the late 16th century the addition of a hornwork with an hexagonal bastion betrayed latent uneasiness about the security of the new gate.

(The Fourth Phase castle of the 20th century largely followed the ground plans of the Second and Third Phases. In so doing much of what could profitably have been used in a more faithful reconstruction to better effect was destroyed. As a result the description of this Second Phase relies upon recent observation and only two sources of information: photographs of the ruins taken at the end of the nineteenth century and the astonishingly complete view and plan of Eilean Donan Castle before it was blown up in 1719.)

*The Photographs*

A group of photographs, including some from the studio of George Washington Wilson, shows the castle as it was in the later 19th century. The most valuable is that of the south elevation looking much more decayed than it was in 1714 but revealing valuable detail.

*The 1714 Survey of the Castle's Second Phase*

Lewis Petit Des Etans (1665?–1720) who carried out the Survey was a Brigadier-General and military engineer. He had worked previously as engineer and surveyor in Ireland and in various military engagements in Europe. In April 1702 he was sent with an expedition to Cadiz and in the following year to Portugal. In 1708 he was captured by the Duc d'Orleans but was released under an exchange. He was then sent to Minorca where he was engaged in building defences around Port Mahon as Lieutenant-Governor of the island. In the same year he was promoted Brigadier-General and appointed full Governor. He returned to England in 1713 and was immediately employed by the Board of Ordnance. On the accession of George I in 1714, Petit was sent to Scotland to assist General Maitland in view of the threatened

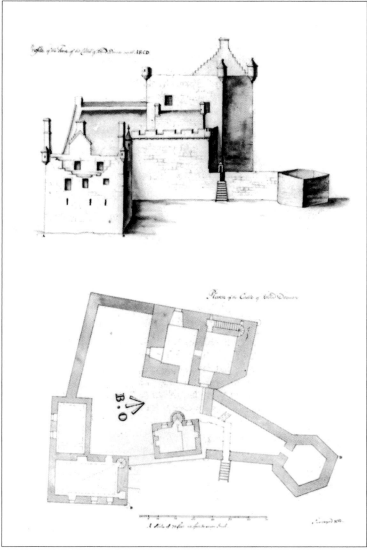

Survey of Eilean Donan in 1714, by Lewis Petit, just five years before it was bombarded by Government vessels which fired the powder magazine and destroyed the castle. Note that the building in front of the tower retains its slated roof and may have been occupied when Petit's survey was made (National Library of Scotland, Crown Copyright).

rising of the clans. His brief was to report on the state of the works at Fort William as well as on other forts and castles in the West of Scotland. It was presumably at this time that he made his survey of the castle at Eilean Donan. Three years later he was commissioned by the Hanoverian Government to produce the design for four barracks from which to subjugate the disaffected Highlands and to determine their siting. One of the proposed new barracks was to be sited at Glenelg and Petit may have returned to confirm the site on the ground. While it was, conceivably, during this later visit that his survey of the castle was made, the former date is the more likely as his specific brief makes clear. Petit's plan bears the Board of Ordnance stamp. It shows a tinted first-floor plan with the associated elevation viewed from the south. The style of drawing is common to that of most accurate ground plans of the period. In contrast, the elevation more resembles those done early in the preceding century where the verticals are produced upwards from the plan, as would be done today, but the horizontals are distorted to form a crude perspective.

A second plan of the castle in advanced ruin was published by MacGibbon and Ross towards the end of the 19th century. This was produced without reference to Petit's drawings. It is impossible to reconcile the two in many instances, particularly in regard to the entry into the courtyard from the west.

The castle shown in Petit's survey is seen to be largely unroofed and dilapidated. Only a rectangular building next to the gate retained its roof, clearly detailed as being slated. By the time MacGibbon and Ross published their description, the castle had been purposely demolished by the detonation of the powder magazine and the little left standing had suffered from two centuries of storm and tempest.

## THE TOWER

During this Second Phase the tower was retained at the north-east corner of a roughly rectangular courtyard approximately 26m. square. Unlike those of Dunvegan and Duntulm where the tower is on the side away from the entrance, the relationship of tower to sea-gate at Eilean Donan had become an adjacent one as a result of the contraction of the castle. Its plan is that of a rectangle some 16.5m. x 12.4m. with walls 3m. in thickness. The south-east corner is dressed back to form a canted face. It is a matter of good fortune that the plans of Petit and MacGibbon and Ross appear to show the basement and first-floor levels respectively.

### The Tower, Ground Floor

From these plans we may deduce that the ground floor lit by narrow loops was barrel-vaulted and divided by a stout masonry wall. Petit's ground plan shows a doorway with square jambs into the western room from the courtyard. Although a doorway is shown between the two rooms it seems the original intention was that the western room could only be approached from the courtyard and the eastern one, a kitchen, down a mural stair in the north wall from the floor above. (In the rebuilding the siting of door and windows was retained but the partition was abbreviated and resited. The stair was not rebuilt and in its place is an alcove.)

*The Tower, First-floor Level*

The whole floor seems to have been taken up by a single room, perhaps the hall, with a narrow screen-lobby at its eastern end into which the outer door opened. The outer door was reached by a wooden external stair and, only later, from the wallhead of the contracted courtyard. The western jamb of this door and the window to its west are shown in a 19th-century photograph. The hall had a mural chamber at its upper end in the thickness of the south-west angle and to the south of a centrally placed window. A doorway opened from the hall into a circular stair running up through the thickness of the north wall, parts of which still survive; to its west a fireplace occupied a site close to the present one. At the eastern end of the north wall another door opened into the lobby at the head of a

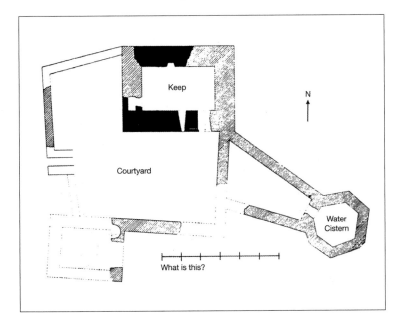

In ignorance of the earlier survey which was not rediscovered until the late 1920s, MacGibbon and Ross bravely attempted a ground plan of the derelict ruin. The result, whilst of interest, was not entirely successful.

The tower during rebuilding in the 1920s. This photograph graphically illustrates the technique of using mural voids to save on labour and weight. The northern (nearer) wall was substantially rebuilt although the southern, farther, wall included surviving upstands from the original structure.

long straight stair down to the basement (?) kitchen. The stair was lit by two loops.

*The Tower, Second-floor Level*

The rooms here were lit by the (?)barred windows shown in Petit's elevation as being on different levels. It may be that these different levels indicate division into at least two rooms.

*The Tower, Third-floor Level*

From the height of wall shown by Petit there must have been a third floor or garret overhead encircled by a parapet walk. Although only three bartizans are shown on his drawing, it is virtually certain that there may have been two more suppressed by the naivety of the perspective. The bartizans at the angle of the east wall still retained their slated roofs terminating in ball finials when Petit's Survey was made. By this time, the main roof had collapsed. As seems to be the case in most of the castles in Skye the gable on the north wall is corbie-stepped. At its apex were substantial chamfer-coped chimney stacks of the type used throughout Scotland. Their size suggests that some contained the three, or four, individual flues from the rooms below.

Again the shortcomings of draughtsmanship have twisted the chimney-gable to make it appear to rise from the north wall rather than in its rightful place on the east wall.

(The 20th-century rebuilding has falsified much of the structure. Walls have been lightened by a honeycombing of passages, closets and wide stairs. Large grouped windows of crudely gothic character have been inserted in places where windows never were before. During the rebuilding the courtyard was lowered to a fast bedrock to give the present attractive ruggedness. This lowering puts the building-levels of the south-west corner out of context.)

## THE CURTAIN WALL OF THE SECOND PHASE

The rectangle enclosed by the shortened curtain was interrupted by later building in a sequence now difficult to determine. Three buildings were constructed abutting or partly overlying the south curtain: one at the south-east angle, the remaining two at its south-west angle. Judging by the character of these structures it seems that the building at the south-east angle, a small block with a stair in a projecting round tourelle, would have been earlier in a scheme of extension than those at the south-west angle. Here there is a structure projecting beyond the line of the south curtain which was subsequently extended northwards over the line of the perimeter to form an L-plan building of the type, seen at Caisteal Camus in Skye, erected early in the 17th century.

*The Second Phase, South Curtain*

At its eastern end is the rectangular building referred to above. This building, some 7.7m. x 5.5m., seems to have fulfilled a variety of functions and may have replaced an earlier structure on a slightly different alignment. From its position just inside the inner entrance one purpose must have been to provide a wall-walk overlooking the inside of the gate. The roof of the circular stair projection provided an essential vantage point in addition to the crenellated wallhead supported on corbels shown by Petit. The first floor of the north front had single windows left and right of the tourelle, on the west there was a single window on the north side of the chimney stack. There appear to have been no windows to south or east. The first floor, the only one

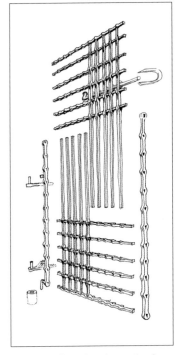

Iron 'yett', a hinged grating made of interlocking bars was commonly employed at the main gate of castles to give added strength and protection to a major point of weakness. In 1893 an iron 'yett' was found in the 'reservoir' of the Phase Three castle. Although this 'yett' almost certainly came from the bastion of the hornwork built onto the castle in the 16th century, it now stands in the tower. The method of its construction is shown here, giving an insight into the complexities of the smith's art.

A 'yett' of strikingly similar form may be seen rehung at Blackness Castle. Those below the rank of baron had to dismantle their yetts by an order of 1606.

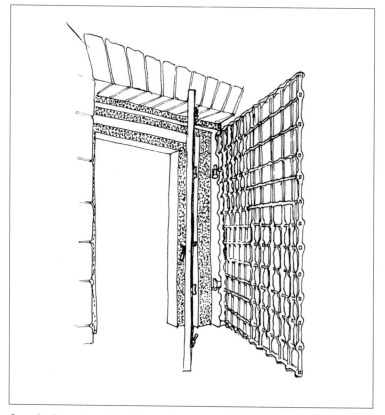

for which a plan of the internal arrangements exists, was divided into two heated rooms separated by a light wooden partition. They were entered by two doors in a lobby at the head of the tourelle. That to the west was the larger. Both were heated by hearths in the west and east gable walls.

It may be inferred that the ground floor entrance to the tourelle stair was within a guard chamber on the ground floor. It may also be assumed that the tourelle stair gave access to the parapet walk. An open bartizan on the south-east angle provided a look-out along the south and east curtain. It was the only part of the castle to retain its slated roof when Petit's Survey was carried out. It was quite common for the gate-house of obsolescent castles to be retained, usually to accommodate the owner's steward or factor, or in other instances as meeting-rooms for a court of petty justice. At Eilean Donan it was perhaps used to accommodate the Reverend Mr. Farquhar until his expulsion in 1650.

(In the 20th century rebuilding this block was extended to the south-west and the original pitched roof truncated to a lead flat. The celebrated dance held in 1715 by Stuart supporters before departing for Sheriffmuir, is reputed to have taken place on one of the castle roofs, but as this was a pitched roof at that time, clearly it cannot have taken place here. A late 19th-century oil painting now hanging in the tower purports to show this event taking place on a leaded roof near a round tower which did not exist at Eilean Donan at that date. The unknown artist reputedly received a description of the event from an eyewitness although the timespan seems to make this most unlikely. During the rebuilding a carriage arch surmounted by armorial panels, used as the present entrance, was driven through the building into the courtyard; at the same time the tourelle 'migrated' 5m. to the west.)

### The Second phase, South-West Angle of the Curtain

At the south-west angle was an L-shaped building erected in two stages. The earlier part, a block 13m. x 8.5m. of three floors and a garret, stood outside the curtain. It is shown in Petit's plan as a rectan-

In dredging out the 'water-tank' in 1893, two pieces of 16th-century artillery were recovered. Subsequently lost, an illustration made in 1913 reveals them to have been brass handguns with spikes for setting the pieces into wooden supports in the wall embrasures.

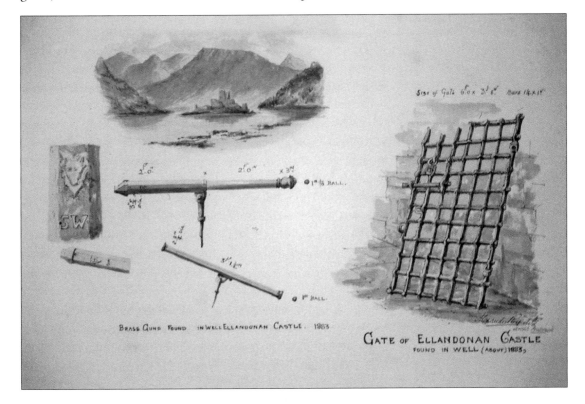

BRASS GUNS FOUND IN WELL ELLANDONAN CASTLE. 1883

GATE OF ELLANDONAN CASTLE
FOUND IN WELL (ABOUT) 1883

gular room approached through a lobby thinly partitioned off from the main room. It was entered from a door cut through the curtain wall at courtyard level. The ground floor actually lay below courtyard level beyond the scarp of the rock plateau. It is plainly indicated to have had a barrel-vault over a single room lit by three narrow loops in the south wall. The external walls of the basement were about 0.3m. thicker than those of the room above. Access to the basement was by a circular mural stair in the north-east angle lit by narrow loops. A clockwise circuit of the first-floor room reveals the following features: a small mural closet in the south-east angle, two smaller windows and a larger in the south wall, a featureless west wall, and a large hearth placed centrally in the main room with a flue emerging at the 'nepus': these small gables carried a dormer-like roof of their own projecting from the main roof, a feature of Scottish building so common as to have their own vernacular name.

The rooms above were lit by windows in the south and north walls and had fireplaces in the west and east gabled ends. The garret overhead necessitated the nepus gable. Running round the wallhead was a crenellated walkway punctuated by bartizans. One which capped the upper run of the circular stair at the north-east angle still retained its finial in 1714, although the main roof of the building had disappeared and the wallhead by then had lost several courses of its stonework. Through this collapsed area may be seen the fireplace below the 'nepus' and a window in the west wall.

Against the west end of the north wall of this building was erected an unheated rectangular building 8.5m. x 6.5m. Its basement was presumably entered down steps from the courtyard not shown on the survey. It was divided by a stout masonry wall near its southern end with a central door from the large northern room into a small closet. This may have been a beer and wine cellar. Petit's plan indicates that the basement walls had a continuous scarcement to support a former vault rather than a timber floor. An open stair led to the room above which was featureless apart from two windows looking out to the west.

(By 1920, the rebuilding had reinstated the barrel vault and made the fenestration of the south-east range more regular, the north-west range was not rebuilt and its floor level now forms part of the lower, paved, courtyard. Its projection beyond the curtain on the west side was retained.)

*The Second Phase, the North-west angle of the Curtain*

Petit shows an open bartizan, presumably one that has lost its cap, at this angle of the parapet walk. The wall was apparently uncrenellated on these sides. His plan clearly shows the overhang of this bartizan.

*The Second Phase, East Curtain*

Immediately to the north of the midpoint of this short stretch of curtain stood the entrance to the castle. Petit's Survey shows only the plain rectangular doorhead peeping over a later wall and the door-

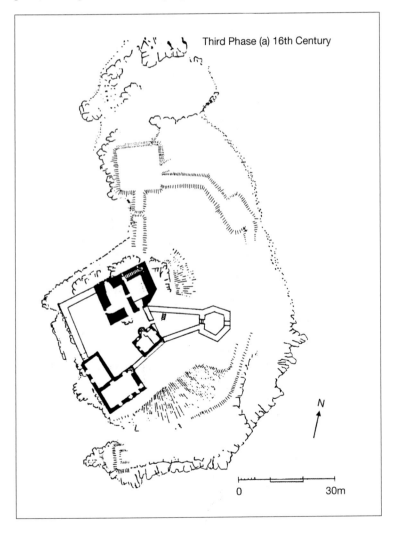

Third Phase (a) 16th Century

0   30m

N

The hornwork added to the east wall in the 16th century created, in effect, a long entrance passage to the inner courtyard which could be effectively covered by firepower. This addition was too ideally suited to the use of artillery to have been built with any other main purpose in mind.

check of its north jamb in plan. At its southern end the curtain had been overlaid by a building on a different alignment.

*The Third Phase, the Hornwork and Hexagonal Water-Tank/Bastion outside the East Curtain*

From the north and south ends of the line of the east curtain were added two convergent walls extending eastwards. This last refinement of the defensive works jutted out beyond the east curtain as a protection of the gate of the Second Phase castle. It terminates in an irregular hexagonal bastion, 11.5m. externally in its longest dimension.

Nowhere is the date of this hornwork recorded. From the character of its masonry alone it seems to date from the late 16th century. Flat-faced rubble, distinctively separated by 'stacked' pinnings, is laid in courses like a crude forerunner of 'Aberdeen Bonding'. Walling of this sort appears within the District in a later 16th-century context at Unish and Caisteal Camus.

*The Hexagonal Bastion*

This is a deceptively simple structure which is functionally, and architecturally, complex. Historically there are no references to the structure which would indicate either its date or purpose. Functionally its principal purpose has been explained as a defence for the fresh water contained within a sinking 10m. deep and 5m. in diameter. However, the need for such a large volume of water over and above the existing provision within the castle can now only be a matter for speculation. Architecturally the form appears unparalleled in contemporary or earlier mediaeval castle construction in the British Isles.

As a piece of defensive architecture it is much more complicated than its present reconstructed form suggests. As it now stands it is difficult to believe the Victorian photographic evidence of a gateway in its ground floor, clearly shown beneath a wide opening flanked by narrower apertures above put-log holes. The latter are suggestive of a late variant of the *bretasche* (a heavy timber, roofed 'balcony' for archers) with the whole construction appearing to represent a variant of the artillery defences seen at Duntulm and perhaps Dunvegan. It may be no accident that during excavation of the reservoir in 1893 two early 16th century pieces of brass artillery were recovered. A drawing, made in 1913 and preserved in the castle, shows them to have been of a type known as 'double hagbutts', measuring 1.29m. and 0.95m. in length and with a bore of 29mm. and 24mm. respectively. The whereabouts of these two pieces is unknown but the muzzle of a third survives in the castle and has a bore of 24mm. The discovery of these pieces supports the late 16th-century date suggested for these outworks.

Through this tower now lay the castle's only outer gate. This was protected by an iron 'yett' or grille, the remains of which were discovered in the reservoir in 1893 and now housed in the tower. It seems that from here the entrance passage was carried over the water reservoir on a timber bridge which, if withdrawn, would have presented an attacker breaching the gate with an impassable water barrier between him and the inner end of the entrance passage. Here a flight of stone steps rose to open out into the funnel-shaped courtyard overlooked by the convergent wall-heads.

Petit shows that access to these was by a flight of (?) wooden steps set against the north curtain, the covered parapet walk here leading onto the bastion and the south curtain wall-head. MacGibbon and Ross state that the bastion was never roofed and certainly it appears without one in Petit's Survey, however neither does Petit show roofs on the tower or south-western range.

*Revision of the Third Phase (b)*

During the 17th century the outer gate was superceded by a less imposing and weaker entrance cut through the wallhead of the southern curtain of the convergent walls and approached by a flight of seven steps. On the west wallhead of this embrasure stood a pillared (?) sentry-box under an ogival roof capped by a finial. Within, a balustraded walk ran northwards for 4.5m. before turning westwards towards the old gate through the east curtain. Just beyond its westward turn the flight of skewed wooden steps leading up the ramp behind the northern most of the convergent courtyard walls was retained.

By this time the castle was in decline and not in a fit state to justify keeping up elaborate defences. The castle was falling into ruin except for the building by the inner gate presumed to have been occupied by the Reverend Mr. Farquhar until his expulsion in 1650. Following the fearful upheavals of 1689 and 1715 and the waning fortunes of the Earldom of Ross, the castle disintegrated more rapidly

In the Third Phase, the doorway through the bastion was superceded by an opening made in the south curtain of the hornwork approached by a rising flight of steps. It was this phase which Petit shows in his Survey of 1714.

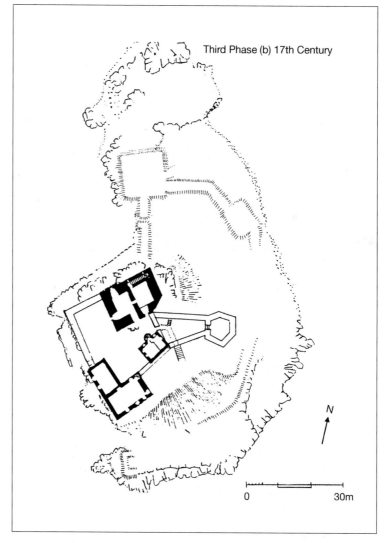

Third Phase (b) 17th Century

0    30m

N

until its final abandonment after the explosion of 1719. Thereafter the vacated part of the earlier courtyard was brought under cultivation and a small bothy built near the shore.

## The Fourth Phase

In the early 20th century the feudal castle was reincarnated, ignoring the informative Survey of 1714 which was only rediscovered shortly before the close of reconstruction. This final structural episode in the history of Eilean Donan has been disregarded here as belonging more to the spirit of Victorian Romantic Mediaevalism than to that of the real castle. The 'new' castle largely followed the ground plan of the Second and Third Phases and, in so doing, obliterated much that could have been used in a more faithful reconstruction.

Between 1912 and 1932 the castle was rebuilt by Lt. Col. MacRae-Gilstrap. This view, taken from the north at an early stage of the work, shows the tower during rebuilding (photograph by Duncan MacPherson. Copyright Mrs. M. Hudson).

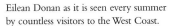

Eilean Donan as it is seen every summer by countless visitors to the West Coast.

# Glossary

BALUSTRADE. A decorative stone or wood openwork parapet with turned or square-section balusters of dwarf columnar form supporting a coping or handrail. Occasionally the balusters may be replaced by openwork panels.

BARREL VAULT. The simplest form of stone vault in the form of a continuous round rubble arch springing from wall to wall. The end walls are vertical rising into the semicircle of the vault.

BARTIZAN. The small overhanging turrets which project from the angles on the top of a tower, or from the parapet or other parts of a building. 'The Bertisene of the steeple' is mentioned in Jamieson's *An Etymological Dictionary of the Scottish Language.*

BASTION. A low tower projecting from the walls of a fortification and rising no higher than the wall to which it is attached. It is common in later fortifications where it was used for artillery.

BROCH. A distinctively Scottish structure currently dated to between the 6th century BC to the 3rd century AD. These towers were built of dry rubble stonework to a circular plan. The walls frequently are found to be waisted and honeycombed by passages and mural chambers. A good and easily accessible example is Dun Beag Broch near Struan in Skye.

CORBEL. A projecting stone giving support to upper masonry projecting beyond the wallface. They are used singly on rare occasions to support a column or bracket, more frequently they are used in rows of 'corbelling' to form a 'corbel table'. A common use was to provide support for the projecting parapet or battlements of a castle wall-head. In the starkly simple castles of Scotland, corbelling is frequently the only decorative motif.

CORBIE-STEPPED. A description of the gable of a building which has its verges protected by a parapet made up of stepped square stones on which the corbie or crow could perch. There is a practical use for the corbie-stepped gable in that the horizontal surfaces provide a ledge for scaffolding-boards during repairs.

CRENELLATED. A word of French derivation meaning battlements but with the added implication that the structure on which they appear is a major fortification (from the mediaeval Royal Licences to Crenellate). It would be wrong to use the term for the ornamental battlements of a church. See MACHICOLATED.

CURTAIN, CURTAIN-WALL. The high crenellated wall of a castle. It may change direction at a tower or bastion or it may be many-sided, unpunctuated by towers. The derivation is from the imagery of a simple window curtain, and was in use from the mid-16th century.

DUN. A prehistoric fort or defensive enclosure usually on a hill-top; it is still a common place-name element in Skye and Lochalsh.

DUNGEON. Its original meaning, from Donjon, is a strong tower or keep. It has also come to mean an underground prison cell of the sort found in the tower of Dunvegan Castle.

EMBRASURE. A window or unglazed opening in masonry. Embrasure in fortifications includes the more strictly applied term 'loop' as well as the gap between the upstands or merlons of crenellation.

ENCEINTE. From the Latin *incingere*, 'to gird in'; in the case of fortifications the enceinte is the area enclosed by the defences.

FARTHING-LAND. Commonly an area of thirty acres (Carew: OED) being a fourth part of a Penny-land. See PENNY-LAND.

FENESTRATION. The arrangement of windows in the facade or a front of a building.

FERMEZ. Literally, farms.

GARRET. A room contrived in the roof-space of a house or castle. It is usually less expensively fitted-up than the rooms on the floors below. The garret corresponds to the 'attic', a floor of lesser rooms above the principal cornice of a classical house.

IRON AGE. In mid-19th century Scandinavia a scholarly approach to the collections in museums resulted in the proposed separation of Prehistory into Stone Age, Bronze Age and Iron Age. Based solely upon technological achievements this division has served well for over a century, but is rapidly diminishing as the complexities of prehistoric societies are becoming better understood. Traditionally, in Northern Scotland, the Iron Age begins around 600–700 BC, and ends around AD 500.

JAMB (1). The 'leg' of a tall 'T-' or 'L-plan' building usually carried up to the top of the structure of which it forms part. The jamb frequently houses the staircase to the rooms in the main block of the plan-form; less frequently it is formed of a series of small rooms one on top of the other reached by mural stairs in another part of the building.

JAMB (2). The side of the rectangular opening or embrasure for a door or fireplace, less frequently that of a window or cupboard. The all-embracing Scottish term 'ingo' or 'ingoes' is more explicit.

LEAD. See SOAKER and VALANCE.

LIME. Lime has been made at Broadford in Skye for many centuries although the kilns, visible as substantial ruins by the shore, are of a 19th-century type. Lime is obtained by burning or calcining limestones, marble or chalk. After the stone has been sufficiently well burned to form 'quick lime' it is usually doused with water to make the burnt masses of stone break down to a powder or slaked lime. During the addition of water considerable heat and consequently steam, is given off and it is at this stage that 'hot lime mortar' is mixed in a proportion of 3 parts of sand to 1 of lime.

Various additives, normally 20 parts of dried clay to 80 parts of lime or less commonly, quantities of powdered coal cinders, make lime more suitable for mortars used in damp conditions.

In some cases lime was actually burnt on site to provide the necessary hot lime for building.

LIME MORTAR. A mixture of sand and lime, the forerunner of modern cement mortar. Its strength and durability varies considerably with the quality and purity of its constituents, in particular the correct burning of the limestone in making lime. The quality of sand or finely parted aggregate used in making the mortar is critical. In Skye the use of well-washed coral sand (which forms the coral beaches north of Dunvegan) has proved to be durable over the centuries. Sea-shore sand is rarely suitable for mortar making and many of the faults seen in local masonry only 80 or 100 years old are attributable to its use.

LIONN-TATH. The Gaelic name for LIME MORTAR.

LOOPS. Small and usually narrow apertures, under lintels, in walls of fortification through which guns or crossbows may be fired. Similar apertures primarily to admit light to mural stairs or chambers but which may still be used for defence.

MAILZ. Yearly rents paid in cash or kind.

NEPUS. A chimney rising from the apex of a gablet (a little gable) on the front of houses. In many cases the flues are constructed in such a way as to allow the construction of centrally placed windows in the gablet immediately below the chimney. The type is as peculiarly Scots as its name.

PARAPET. A low wall erected at the side of a wall-head or wall-walk for protection from missiles or to prevent people from falling off.

PENNY-LAND. Land valued at a 'penny' a year in rent or other exaction. *Peinduin*, the 'pennyland of the fort', is so-called from the Norse valuation at a penny-weight's worth of silver in rent. 'Penny-land' later became a description of its extent and value for translation into more modern currencies.

QUOIN. Quoins are the squared stones forming the corners of the walling of a square or angled building. From the late 16th century 'side-alternate' quoins of regularly sized and finished rectangular blocks replaced the haphazard sizing of earlier work; the long sides of the blocks alternated with the shorter ends, one above the other, to give a neat finish to the corners of the rougher wall-stone.

SOAKER. A sheet of lead laid beneath the sloping verge of slating and mortared into a cut chace, or groove, in the adjacent walling to prevent rain driving through the gap. A valance is a sheet of lead mortared into a chace some 50mm. above the soaker and dressed down the wall-face onto the slates to give a virtually impenetrable seal.

SCREEN LOBBY. The mediaeval house commonly had a 'screens' passageway across its width between the kitchen and the hall; the front and rear entrance doorways were sited at the ends with internal communicating doors in the side-walls. Where halls were built above ground floor level the motif was the basis for improvisation. The internal lobby, or 'spere', was an inner porch, usually framed in wainscot boarding, with doors to cut down draughts. The 'screen lobby' combines many of the functions of both.

SIDE-ALTERNATE. See QUOIN.

TACK. A Tack was a form of lease of land or property. The lease was frequently renewable for long periods with some review of rent at intervals. The holder of a Tack, the Tacksman, was frequently a blood relative of the landlord and in many cases the financial arrangements were favourable to the Tacksman. Where the property involved was extensive, the Tacksman could sublet divisions of the land, more often than not at a rent considerably more than he paid himself. The Tacksman's tenants had little or no legal title to their holdings, or to the buildings they might erect on them, and they could be evicted summarily, particularly at the cessation of a Tack. The insecurity of such sub-tenure was particularly acute during the 18th- and 19th-century Clearances, when whole communities were evicted to clear the land for the more profitable sheep.

TOURELLE. A small tower of circular plan, often containing a stair or, less frequently, closets, abutting and rising higher than the building it served.

UNDERCROFT. The room, usually stone-vaulted, lying beneath the great upper-halls of substantial houses built before the 16th century. In rich town- or manor-houses they were of considerable elaboration, with columns under carved capitals and compartmented vaulting. In Romanesque houses (11th or 12th century) the undercroft served as an auxiliary hall more frequently that it was used for storage.

VALANCE: See SOAKER.

VOUSSOIRS. The tapered stones forming the sides of an arch, left and right of the keystone.

WADSET. A form of land tenure where the landlord leased land in consideration of his debt to the leaseholder. The lease was terminated on the repayment of the debt by the landlord and the property reverted to him.

WINDOWS. It has been said, with some truth, that 'architecture is dated by the holes in it', meaning a building's doors and windows. The major changes in the historic period discussed in this book was the substitution, from the later 16th century, of larger wooden windows with a hinged opening for the smaller masonry apertures with fixed leaded lights stiffened by iron saddlebars. The upper part of such windows was frequently glazed but the lower part was closed by wooden shutters. The introduction of the sash window, now so frequently seen in Scottish castles, was not until after 1700 as a replacement of the wooden mullion (upright, central frame member) and transome (wooden cross-bar) type. Of the mullioned stone window of the earlier period, with or without tracery, there is no remaining example if such did indeed exist.